Hiking Georgia
ATLANTA

Hiking Georgia
ATLANTA

A Guide to 30 Great Hikes Close to Town

Don Pfitzer and Jimmy Jacobs
Photography by Polly Dean

FALCONGUIDES

GUILFORD, CONNECTICUT
HELENA, MONTANA

FALCONGUIDES®

An imprint of Rowman & Littlefield
Falcon, FalconGuides, and Outfit Your Mind are registered trademarks of Rowman & Littlefield.

Distributed by NATIONAL BOOK NETWORK

Copyright © 2015 by Rowman & Littlefield
Maps: Design Maps Inc. © Rowman & Littlefield

British Library Cataloguing-in-Publication Information available

Library of Congress Cataloging-in-Publication Data

Pfitzer, Donald W.
  Hiking Georgia. Atlanta : guide to 30 great hikes close to town / Donald W. Pfitzer and Jimmy Jacobs ; photography by Polly Dean.
    pages cm
  Includes index.
    ISBN 978-1-4930-1315-9 (pbk.) – ISBN a9781493014392 (e-book) 1. Hiking—Georgia—Atlanta Metropolitan Area—Guidebooks. 2. Family recreation—Georgia—Atlanta Metropolitan Area—Guidebooks. 3. Atlanta Metropolitan Area (Ga.)—Guidebooks. I. Jacobs, Jimmy. II. Title. III. Title: Atlanta, guide to 30 great hikes close to town.
  GV199.42.G462A857 2015
  796.5109758'231—dc23

2015009026

∞™ The paper used in this publication meets the minimum requirements of American National Standard for Information Sciences—Permanence of Paper for Printed Library Materials, ANSI/NISO Z39.48-1992.

CONTENTS

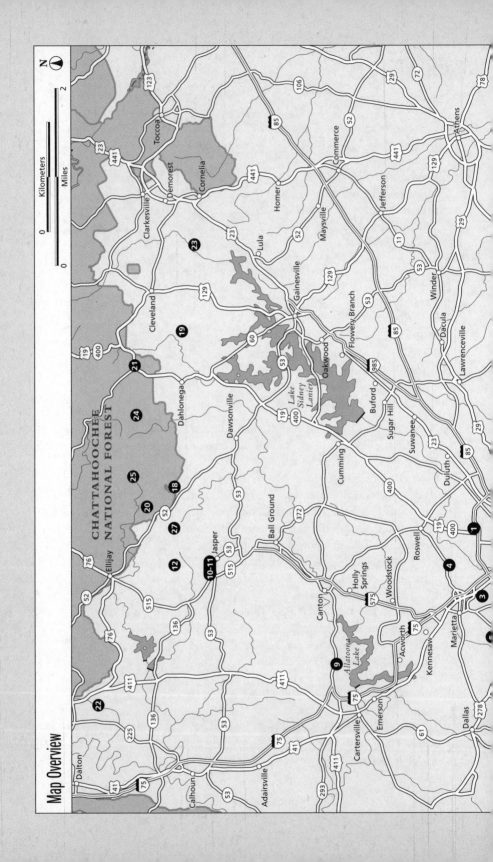

Map Overview

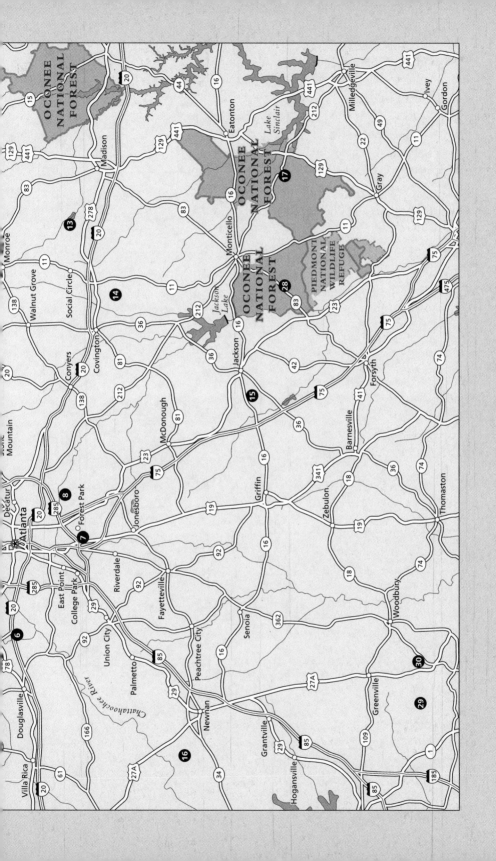

Introduction

Atlanta's vibrant city life, combined with its easy access to mountains, woodlands, and waterways, makes it one of America's most livable cities. Plenty of accessible parks, green spaces, and woodlands surrounding the city make it easy for residents and tourists alike to find suitable hiking destinations close by. This book features thirty varied hikes in close proximity to the city, from easy walks along quiet nature trails to more strenuous treks through mountainous terrain. There are destinations to suit every interest—from urban paths along gorgeous waterways to historic sites just outside the city's limits. This guide will help you find the right hike for your interests and skill level.

Zero Impact Hiking

Reward the thousands of volunteers who create and help maintain the trails and allow those who follow your footsteps to enjoy their own wilderness experience by leaving an area as pristine as you found it—or better. The following guidelines can help ensure enjoyable hiking experiences for years to come:

- Pack it in; pack it out. Few things are more irritating than finding aluminum cans, candy wrappers, and other litter along the trail. Pack out what you pack in—and carry an extra garbage bag on hikes for carting out litter left behind by others.

- Stay on the trail. Designated paths limit the impact on natural areas. Taking shortcuts or straying off the blazed trail can cause damage to sensitive areas that can take years to heal.

Leaving no trace should be the goal of every hiker passing along the trails.

- Respect other trail users. If you are on a multiuse trail that allows horses, remember that they have the right-of-way. Step aside quietly, off the trail if necessary, and let horse and rider pass. Although hikers generally have right-of-way on trails shared with mountain bikers, it's probably best to yield for safety's sake—especially on narrow or steep trail sections.

  To learn more about leaving no trace, visit www.LNT.org.

Be Prepared

Should I Drink from That Stream?

In Georgia the answer is no—unless the water has been treated by boiling, filtered with a reliable filter/purifier, or treated with an effective chemical purifier.

From the mountains to the sea, there is no real shortage of water in Georgia. However, water quality can be a problem. Day hikers should bring sufficient water for drinking unless potable water is known to be available. All Georgia state parks and most USDA Forest Service campgrounds and recreation areas have potable running water. Only occasionally will you find yourself several miles from surface water from a spring, stream, or lake. On long trails like the Appalachian Trail, water sources are marked both by signs and on trail maps. Again, this water must be treated before it is considered safe to drink.

No matter how pretty and inviting a stream may look, you should never drink the water without first boiling, filtering, or chemically treating it.

Do not drink water directly from streams, no matter how remote they are or how clean and pure they seem to be.

First Aid

A first-aid kit should be part of every hiker's backpack, whether you're on a day hike or a longer trek. There are many good lightweight, compact kits on the market. Be especially prepared to take care of hike-spoiling blisters by carrying moleskin, gauze, and tape or adhesive bandages.

Dangers

Wear sunscreen (SPF 15 or higher), protective clothing, a wide-brimmed hat, and sunglasses when you are hiking. If you get sunburn, treat the area with aloe vera gel, and protect the area from further sun exposure. Don't let overcast skies fool you into thinking you're safe—you can burn even when you cannot see the sun.

Bear encounters are extremely rare, except at campsites where garbage has been allowed to accumulate. At some shelters along the Appalachian Trail, where hundreds of campers a year spend the night, bears may become night visitors looking for food. You will seldom, if ever, see black bears while walking trails. They will usually run before you get close enough to see them.

Stinging insects represent the greatest and most frequently encountered danger on Georgia's trails. Wasps build nests on bridge handrails or under benches. Running the hand against a wasp nest or brushing against a nest hanging on low vegetation can cause stings that are fortunately only temporarily painful for most people. However, for those few who are allergic to bee and wasp stings, the problem can be life threatening. Know your sensitivity—or the sensitivity of anyone in

The fields and woodlands of Georgia are home to a staggering array of insect life.

your hiking party—and prepare for it. Know what to do in the event of a sting, and carry the appropriate antihistamines or other medication in your first-aid kit to use immediately if stung.

Chiggers (red bugs), mosquitoes, biting flies, and gnats are common throughout the state. They are most annoying during the warmer months and during twilight and nighttime hours. In parts of southern Georgia and in the coastal counties, mosquitoes can be very annoying during the day. Be sure to use an effective all-around repellent. The most effective repellents contain at least 30 percent DEET. Other repellents are available for those who are sensitive to DEET, including young children.

Ticks are another problem in Georgia. These bugs can transmit two diseases: Lyme disease and Rocky Mountain spotted fever. Lyme disease occurs throughout Georgia but is most prevalent in the southern two-thirds of the state. It is transmitted by the tiny deer tick. The larger wood tick can transmit spotted fever. A few spotted fever cases are reported each year, while Lyme disease has become much more prevalent.

The best way to avoid ticks on the trail is to use an effective repellent before you head out. DEET is effective against ticks. Another highly effective repellent, which also kills ticks, is Permanone. It should not be applied directly to the skin but is very effective when applied to clothes and footwear before going into tick-infested areas. Wear a long-sleeved shirt and long pants tucked into your footwear. Examine yourself carefully immediately after a day hike and once a day or more on longer hikes. The tiny deer tick nymphs, the most active carrier of the Lyme disease spirochete, may be picked up even during mild winter months in Central and South Georgia.

Removing an attached tick in the first 8 to 10 hours is important. To remove the tick, use forceps or tweezers to grasp the tick as close to the skin as possible; gently but firmly pull the tick away, trying not to leave its mouthparts in the skin. Squeezing the tick's body can act like a syringe, forcing the tick's body fluids into your body and increasing the potential for Lyme disease. In about half the cases of Lyme disease, redness occurs around the bite and may take on a bull's-eye appearance. This should be reported to a doctor as soon as possible. Treated early, Lyme disease is quickly cured.

Venomous snakes in Georgia run from the small, secretive coral snake to the eastern diamondback rattlesnake, our largest North American snake. The coral snake occurs in both dry and moist sandy-loam areas of the southern third of Georgia. The timber rattlesnake occurs throughout the state from the mountains through the Coastal Plain. It may be called the canebrake rattlesnake in the southern part of the state. Coral snakes and rattlesnakes are rarely seen.

Most Georgia snakes are harmless and quite beneficial to the ecosystem.

The copperhead is the state's most common venomous snake.

Both the northern and southern copperheads occur in Georgia. The larger southern copperhead is found throughout the Piedmont, along the fall line, and in the Coastal Plain. The northern copperhead is generally found in the Piedmont and all the mountain regions.

The cottonmouth, or water moccasin, is found from the fall line south throughout the Coastal Plain along streams, river swamps, and marshes.

Many new hikers in Georgia seem to fear snakes more than other hazards along the trail, carrying snakebite kits with little knowledge of how to use them. Most of these kits have blades to cut the fang puncture, a tourniquet, disinfectant, and other things—none of which are practical first aid for a venomous snakebite. The best first aid for venomous snakebite is get to medical help as soon as possible.

To reduce your risk of snakebite, don't put your foot or hand anywhere without looking first. Be cautious stepping over logs. Keep your hands and feet out of cavities around boulders. Since many snakes are nocturnal, carry and use a flashlight if you need to walk on trails at night during warm weather. Even nonvenomous snakebites can be painful and prone to infection.

Poison ivy is present on many trails in Georgia. It is most obvious in late spring and throughout the summer months. Learn to recognize it and avoid it: "Leaves of three, let it be." Washing exposed skin with soap and water as soon as possible after contact is the best way to prevent irritation.

Hypothermia has been called the number-one killer among all outdoor injuries. The lowering of internal body temperature from exposure to cold, wind, rain, or immersion in cold water, hypothermia can occur even when outdoor temperatures are not very cold. Learn to recognize the symptoms and know that injuries increase the risk of hypothermia. First signs include shivering, followed by no shivering, disorientation, and confusion. Later the person may appear apathetic and moody. As hypothermia becomes more advanced, the victim may lapse into a coma.

The first step in treatment of hypothermia, after making all possible arrangements to get the person to expert medical attention, is to reduce heat loss. Get the victim out of the wind and into dry clothes and/or a windproof shell like a poncho or space blanket (a good addition to your first-aid kit). Pay special attention to covering the head and back of the neck with a cap, hat, or anything windproof and warm. Next try to produce heat in the body core. If the victim can drink, give him/her warm, sweet fluids—not alcohol.

After applying dry clothing and a windproof outer covering, get the victim walking, with support if necessary. Exercise is the best way to improve internal organ heat. If you are alone and recognize hypothermia, drink hot fluids like sweet hot chocolate, get into dry clothes, protect yourself from the wind, and keep moving. Movement is crucial. Obviously, it's important to be able to recognize the condition before you become disoriented or confused.

Planning Your Trip

For safety's sake, always leave your hike itinerary with someone before you head out. It should include where you will be hiking, where you will park, your estimated time of completing the trip, and whom to contact if necessary. "Trail Contacts" for each trail description list phone numbers and websites that can be used to contact park personnel should emergencies arise.

Packing a rain jacket is wise because Georgia's changeable weather can bring clouds rolling in.

There are registers on the Appalachian Trail (AT) at the Springer Mountain trailhead (hike 12) and at many of the shelters. It is a good idea to leave pertinent information at these points. For the AT and some other trails, you must register with the appropriate land-managing agencies.

The Coosa Backcountry Trail, which originates at Vogel State Park (hike 25) and the Pine Mountain Trail at F. D. Roosevelt State Park (hike 29) are other trails requiring registration to obtain a free permit to hike or camp along these paths.

Comfortable clothing and footwear will do more to make a hike pleasant than almost anything else. The great variety of hiking and walking situations makes it impossible to cover all personal needs, but two important ones are to dress in layers and dress for safety in hunting season. The first allows you to remove or add layers to suit the weather. The second involves wearing blaze orange to make you visible to hunters in the area.

Everyone seems to have a different idea about what type of footwear to wear for hiking. Footwear boils down to personal preference, but it should be sturdy and supportive. Many people still wear good leather boots for serious hiking; others prefer lighter-weight boots with breathable, water-resistant fabrics. The best advice for the beginner is to visit a good outdoor outfitter and try on several styles before finally deciding.

There are many types and styles of backpacks. For day hiking, the smaller daypack type is all you need. It should fit and have padded shoulder and hip pads. Make sure they are wide enough to be comfortable. The pack should have external pockets for easy access to items like camera, water, and maps. External

Wearing a blaze orange cap is a wise decision when hiking during hunting seasons.

straps are handy to lash things like a jacket or poncho. The main bag should be large enough for lunch or other bulky things. Don't burden yourself with a daypack that is too large. You may find that a fanny pack or a photo vest will carry all you want or need.

Hiking in Georgia is a year-round activity, with many good hiking days in winter. Wintertime snow and cold or freezing rain in the mountains and spring and summer showers and thunderstorms throughout the state are about the only weather conditions that hamper your comfort on the trail. Fall weather is best, and September through November is the most popular time to hike.

Be aware of changing weather conditions. If thunderstorms are in the forecast, recognize that lightning in forest cover can be dangerous. Do not hike along ridgetops and on mountain crests with large exposed rock formations during electrical storms, especially with metal-frame backpacks.

Wintertime hikes can be especially beautiful in the limited snow that falls in the Georgia mountains. Plans for snow hiking should include adequate footwear and clothing to tolerate the cold, wet conditions in case an emergency occurs. Being wet and cold invites hypothermia, a potentially life-threatening condition.

Navigation

Maps

US Geological Survey (USGS) 7.5-minute series topographic quadrangles, scale 1:24,000, referred to in the text for each hike, are the best and most dependable maps for long hikes and wilderness backpack trip planning. Learn how to read them, and then learn to rely on them for keeping oriented on the trail. This is especially important for any cross-country hikes requiring good orienteering techniques. These USGS quadrangles are available at most outdoor shops that cater to hikers' needs. They can be purchased from the US Geological Survey National Mapping Division at USGS.gov/pubprod.

Page-size maps of the trails in most of the state parks can be obtained free of charge from the respective parks or downloaded from www.gastateparks.org. These maps may not be to scale, but they will keep you oriented. They also can help you take advantage of all the special natural and historical points of interest along the way.

The Georgia Appalachian Trail Club offers a small-scale map with helpful hints for hiking the AT. The *Appalachian Trail Guide to North Carolina–Georgia* contains maps, trail mileages, water and shelter locations, and side trails; it can be purchased at hiking and backpacking outfitters and stores or from the Appalachian Trail Conservancy, www.atctrailstore.org.

The comprehensive website of the Benton MacKaye Trail Association (www .bmta.org) contains excellent information on this newest of the long trails in Georgia and other trails throughout the mountains of northeast Georgia.

Compass

The compass is probably the most valuable tool you can have to stay properly oriented in unfamiliar terrain. Some characteristics to look for in a compass are a rectangular base with detailed scales, a liquid-filled protective housing, a sighting line on the mirror, and luminous arrows. Learn to use the compass so well that you don't even think about dis-believing it.

Global Positioning System (GPS)

This is possibly the most useful navigation gadget to come along for the serious hiker. As with all such tools, you must learn how to use a GPS accurately. Most brands are sold with good instructions that anyone with computer experience should be able to master. Practice

Modern GPS units add a new dimension to navigating through the woodlands.

with your GPS until you are comfortable with it before you go into the backcountry on an extended hike. If you use a mapping program, you can come home from a hike and download the GPS data into your computer for a permanent record of your hike.

All GPS products use the same satellite support base. The real difference among products is in the quality of satellite reception. All are limited when in mountainous terrain with deep valleys and under dense deciduous tree cover. (Deciduous tree leaves are notorious for diffusing radio signals.) Of course as time passes, technology is catching up with those problems

The trail tracks used to create the maps in this volume were made with Garmin GPSMAP 62stc or touch-screen Garmin RINO 665t units. In more than 500 miles of trekking, the units lost satellite contact only once. That occurred in the bottom of a deep, solid rock grotto in Cloudland Canyon State Park.

Hiking with Children

Children learn by example. Hiking trips are excellent opportunities to teach young ones to tread lightly and minimize their imprint upon the environment. Many state parks have nature trails ideal for beginning hikers and offer interpretive programs for children and adults conducted by park naturalists and program specialists.

Kids can enjoy the backcountry as much as their parents, but they see the world from a different perspective. It's the little things adults barely notice that are so special to children. Bugs scampering across the trail, spider webs dripping with morning dew, lizards doing push-ups on a trailside boulder, skipping rocks on a lake, watching sticks run the rapids of a mountain stream, exploring animal tracks in the sand—these are but a few of the natural wonders kids will enjoy while hiking backcountry trails.

To make the trip fun for the kids, let the young ones set the pace. Until they get older and are able to keep up with you, forget about that 30-mile trek to your favorite backcountry campsite. Instead, plan a destination that is only a mile or two from the trailhead. Kids tire quickly and become easily sidetracked, so don't be surprised if you don't make it to your destination.

Hikers with Special Needs

State and federal land management agencies in Georgia are putting a great deal of effort into making their facilities accessible to visitors with special needs. A number of parks and other areas covered in the following chapters have wheelchair-accessible paths or trails. These are highlighted where relevant.

Volunteering

Georgia is home to several hiking clubs and conservation organizations that are involved in hiking. Some devote a large amount of their time to trail maintenance. The Georgia Appalachian Trail Club, Benton MacKaye Trail Club, and the Pine Mountain Trail Association plan regular outings to work on these trails. The Georgia

Department of Natural Resources, USDA Forest Service, National Park Service, and US Fish and Wildlife Service also welcome volunteers who are willing to help maintain and mark trails. The forest service's "Adopt-A-Trail" program is especially suited to volunteer efforts.

Using This Guide

Degrees of difficulty are based on the grade or incline of the trail. A flat trail with very little elevation change is designated easy whether it is 0.5 mile or 5.0 miles long. A moderate hike will have a moderately steep grade for extended distances. A strenuous trail may have steep grades for 0.5 mile or more. Degree of difficulty may be expressed with two or three ratings, as easy to moderate or moderate with strenuous stretches. Where a trail is uneven and footing is more difficult because of boulders or other obstacles, this will be discussed in the description of the hike.

All but a very few trails described in this guide are marked in some fashion. A paint mark (blaze) on a tree is the most frequent trail marker. One trail will be marked or blazed throughout with one color paint. In a state park with several different trails, a different color may be used for each trail. A few trails are marked with a white 3- to 4-inch diamond-shaped piece of metal nailed to trees and posts along the trail instead

Blazes can be metal or plastic strips nailed to trees, or they may simply be painted on the trunk.

of paint blazes. Carsonite stakes, flat fiberglass posts about 4 inches wide and 4 to 5 feet tall, are being used to mark some trailheads and occasionally along some trails. These are less vulnerable to vandalism and are marked with decals designating trail use and activities not permitted on the trail.

It has become standard to mark sudden changes in direction of a trail with two blaze marks, one above the other on the same tree. Most trails are marked so that you should not travel more than 0.25 mile without seeing a blaze. Because of dense vegetation, state park and many USDA Forest Service trails are marked with paint blazes much more frequently. Where two trails occasionally join for a distance, two colors or types of blazes are used until the trails separate again.

Map Legend

Transportation

≡⟨85⟩≡ Interstate Highway

≡⟨76⟩≡ US Highway

⊂⟨28⟩⊃ State Highway

≡⟨236⟩≡ Forest/Local Road

= = = = Unpaved Road

||||||||| Boardwalk

Trails

▪▪▪▪▪▪ Featured Trail

------ Trail

--⟨A⟩-- Appalachian Trail

Water Features

 Body of Water

 River/Creek

σ⌐ Spring

≶ Waterfall

Land Management

----- State Line

 National Forest

 State Park

 Wilderness/Recreation Area

Symbols

⇐ Boat Ramp

‿ Bridge

▲ Campground

▲ Campsite (backcountry)

⊛ Capital

— Dam

⸑ Gate

▲ Mountain Peak/Summit

🅿 Parking

⤬ Pass/Gap

🎌 Picnic Area

■ Point of Interest/Structure

🏠 Ranger Station

♟ Tower

○ Town

❶ Trailhead

❺ Trail Direction

🚻 Restroom

❀ Viewpoint/Overlook

❓ Visitor/Information Center

1 Island Ford Trail

The 297-acre Island Ford Unit of the Chattahoochee River National Recreation Area (CRNRA) has been retained in as natural a condition as possible for almost a century, first by the original private owners and later by the National Park Service. The mature hardwood forest at this site is a fine example of what the Piedmont area of Georgia might have looked like before it was cleared and developed.

This is a great natural area, especially for a highly residential portion of metropolitan Atlanta, to find a variety of spring and summer wildflowers, trees, and wildlife. The area also contains a number of rock shelters along the river, as well as shoals within the stream.

Visitors use the site as start or finish points for paddling trips on the Chattahoochee, for picnicking along the shore, or wading in pursuit of rainbow and brown trout.

The unit contains a system of interconnected trails, none of which bear names. All the trails have signs with maps at junctions and are easy to follow. The featured hike is a combination of several of these paths, creating a double-loop trek beginning and ending at the parking lot at the CRNRA office. The trail combination enables you to see a wide variety of habitats in a relatively small area.

Start: At the information sign in front of the CRNRA office
Distance: 2.2-mile double loop
Hiking time: About 1–1.5 hours
Difficulty: Easy to moderate
Trail surface: Mostly clay or sandy loam
Best season: Mar–Dec
Other trail users: Anglers
Canine compatibility: Leashed dogs permitted
Land status: Chattahoochee River National Recreation Area

Nearest town: Roswell
Fees and permits: Daily parking fee
Maps: USGS Sandy Springs; page-size map available from the park service office or from www.nps.gov./chat
Trail contacts: National Park Service, Chattahoochee River National Recreation Area, 1978 Island Ford Pkwy., Atlanta 30350; (678) 538-1200; www.nps.gov./chat

Finding the trailhead: From I-285 take exit 27 and follow SR 400 north 5 miles to exit 6 (North Ridge Road). Turn right and go back across SR 400. Turn right at the traffic light to Roberts Road. Go 1.2 miles to the National Park Service entrance sign; turn right on Island Ford Parkway. The trailhead is 1.1 miles ahead, where the parkway dead-ends at the CRNRA office. Trailhead GPS: N33 59.234'/W84 19.502'

The Hike

The Island Ford Trail provides a pleasant hike in a mature hardwood forest and along the shoals of the Chattahoochee River. The path takes you through all the habitat types with flat, easy walks and moderate climbs in the hilly upland. It is almost all shaded during the warm months and an open forest canopy in winter.

The trail parallels the Island Ford shoals on the river.

Start from the information sign in front of the CRNRA office, following the paved pathway around the left side of the building. Once past the office the trail reaches the junction where the second smaller loop on the trail closes from the right. Turn left here and descend the steps toward the river.

As you climb down the hill, a picnic pavilion with a massive stone barbecue pit appears on the left. This structure predates the park service acquisition of the property. Continue down to a trail junction at the foot of the hill. The trail to the left follows a small stream up toward a small lake. This moist cove is full of spleenworts and Christmas ferns. The forest canopy is composed of dogwoods, redbuds, yellow poplar, white oak, American beech, maples, sweet gums, and loblolly pines.

From the junction turn right and follow the creek to the riverbank and another junction. The smaller loop of the trail goes to the right here; turn left across a footbridge and walk downstream along the river. Quickly you pass another trail joining on the left. This one also leads uphill to the lake.

For the next 0.2 mile the trail hugs the riverbank offering views of the shoals and the island that splits the river into two channels. During most seasons Canada geese, kingfishers, and mallard ducks are present in or over the water. Water-tolerant river birch, ironwood, sycamore, and red maple trees grow right to the riverbank. Mosses, liverworts, and ferns help stabilize the bank.

This is also a popular stretch with wading anglers. In the warmer months expect to see swimmers and rafters on the water as well.

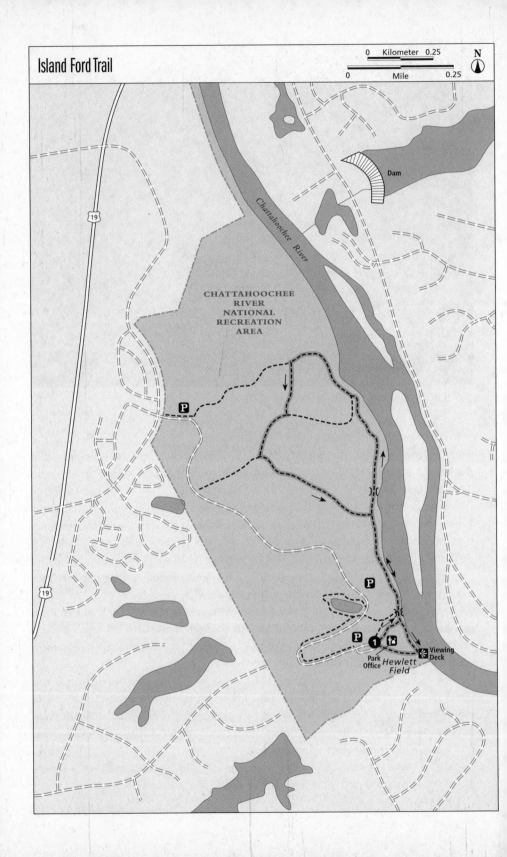

Island Ford Trail

0   Kilometer   0.25

0   Mile   0.25

N

19

Chattahoochee River

CHATTAHOOCHEE
RIVER
NATIONAL
RECREATION
AREA

Dam

P

P

P

1

Park
Office

Hewlett
Field

Viewing
Deck

The next trail junction is the beginning of the larger loop on the path. A large rock shelter is on the left of the intersection. Continue straight, following the river. The path crosses a footbridge and then passes two more rock shelters before reaching yet another trail entering from the left. This is one of several connectors that shortcut the larger loop.

Finally, at the next trail junction, the main path turns left to leave the river. Be careful at this point, for a fisherman's path continues down the riverbank. The trail gradually bends to turn back south, climbing through a switchback as it gains elevation. Once you're headed south, a trail coming down from a parking lot on Island Ford Parkway enters from the right. Continue straight at this junction. When the trail reaches its highest point on the ridge, a trail forks off to the right to another parking area. Bear to the left at this intersection and begin descending the ridge.

Just prior to closing the large loop, the trail follows along the top of a mini gorge through which Summerbrook Creek tumbles toward the river.

At the close of the loop at the intersection by the rock shelter, turn right and retrace your steps upriver to cross the footbridge at the junction where the smaller loop begins. The trail now passes between a rock outcrop and the river. A wooden handrail is on the river side of the path along this stretch. The trail next comes out into the open at the grassy Hewett Field. This is an activity area that features a canoe and raft launch.

Turn sharply to the right and begin climbing up to the close of the smaller loop behind the CRNRA office. At the junction, turn left on the paved walk to arrive back at the trailhead.

Miles and Directions

0.0 Begin down the paved path to the junction at the close of the little loop and turn left.

0.1 Pass the historic picnic pavilion and lake trail junction, and reach the intersection at the river; turn left across the footbridge and pass the second lake trail.

0.3 Reach the beginning of the larger loop and continue straight; a rock shelter is on the left.

0.4 Cross a footbridge over a feeder stream and pass two more rock shelters.

0.7 Pass a connecting trail on the left.

0.8 The trail now turns left to begin climbing away from the river.

1.0 Go straight at the intersection with the trail from the Island Ford Parkway parking lot.

1.3 Reach the highest point on the trail and another trail on the right from Island Ford Parkway.

1.8 Close the larger loop and turn upriver to the right.

2.0 To begin the smaller loop, continue straight through the trail junction, quickly passing beneath a rock outcrop on the right.

2.1 Turn sharply right at Hewlett Field and climb toward the CRNRA office.

2.2 Turn left at the close of the smaller loop and arrive back at the trailhead.

2 East Palisades Trail

The East Palisades Unit comprises 393 acres of hardwood forest with rock outcrops, ravines, and a narrow river floodplain. The East Palisades Trail has a number of connecting trails in the interior of its loop. The main trail and most of these connectors all have blue blazes.

Roughly 5 miles of forest footpaths wind along the steep bluffs overlooking the east side of the river. Only short sections of the East Palisades Trail are steep and strenuous for hiking. The elevation change from the river to the highest point in the unit is about 290 feet.

An observation deck provides a panoramic view of the river shoals from the top of the bluff. River boatmen in the eighteenth and nineteenth centuries called these rapids Devils Race Course Shoals. They named the granite palisades the Devil's Stairsteps.

The featured hike is a combination of the 2.8-mile East Palisades Trail loop and 1.0-mile one-way Cabin Creek Trail.

See map page 18.
Start: At Indian Trail parking area
Distance: 4.6-mile out and back, with a loop at the beginning
Hiking time: About 3–4 hours
Difficulty: Mostly moderate, with short strenuous stretches
Trail surface: Dirt and sandy loam
Best season: Year-round
Other trail users: Joggers
Canine compatibility: Leashed dogs permitted
Land status: Chattahoochee River National Recreation Area (CRNRA)

Nearest town: Roswell
Fees and permits: Daily parking fee
Schedule: Park opens dawn to dusk, year-round
Maps: USGS Sandy Springs; page-size map available from the National Park Service office and from www.nps.gov/chat
Trail contacts: National Park Service, Chattahoochee River National Recreation Area, 1978 Island Ford Pkwy., Atlanta 30350; (770) 399-8070; www.nps.gov/chat

Finding the trailhead: Exit I-285 at Northside Drive (exit 22). Follow this residential road south to Indian Trail. Turn right and go 0.5 mile to the dead end in the parking area at the trailhead. Trailhead GPS: N33 53.043'/W84 26.213'

The Hike

Beginning at the Indian Trail parking area, the path follows an old roadbed for a few yards before dropping down in a series of switchbacks to Whitewater Creek and the river. A bridge on the left crosses Long Island Creek to an alternate trailhead at the Whitewater Creek parking area (Trailhead GPS: N33 52.706' / W84 26.510').

At the river, the path is only a few feet from the bank. This is a good place to look for tracks of muskrats, beavers, raccoons, minks, and other mammals using the river's

A panorama of Devils Race Course Shoals is offered from the observation deck.

edge. The exposed rocks visible when the river is running low, or the whitewater when the river is up, are Long Island Shoals and Thornton Shoals. Large patches of shrubs, switch cane, and honeysuckle grow in the wet areas along the bank. Through here you cross two short boardwalks and one footbridge.

After crossing a second footbridge over Charlies Trapping Creek, you reach the first of a number of trails intersecting from the right. At each of these, take the path to the left.

The path soon begins the climb up along the palisades. This is the steepest portion of the trail.

Once on the top of the high bluff you pass a wintertime overlook, and then the trail turns left down to the observation deck. From the deck you get a grand view of the river and appreciate the height of the bluffs.

The main channel of the river below going through Devils Race Course is not natural. It was blasted out with dynamite to allow for the passage of flatboats in the 1800s.

Exiting the overlook, you turn left. Shortly you pass the junction with the Cabin Creek Trail and turn left. Descending a ridge from the junction, the path goes through a beautiful mature hardwood forest of large yellow poplars, white oaks, chestnut oaks, and an occasional deciduous magnolia with exceptionally large leaves. Orange flame azaleas, honeysuckle, and mountain laurel bloom along the trail in the spring.

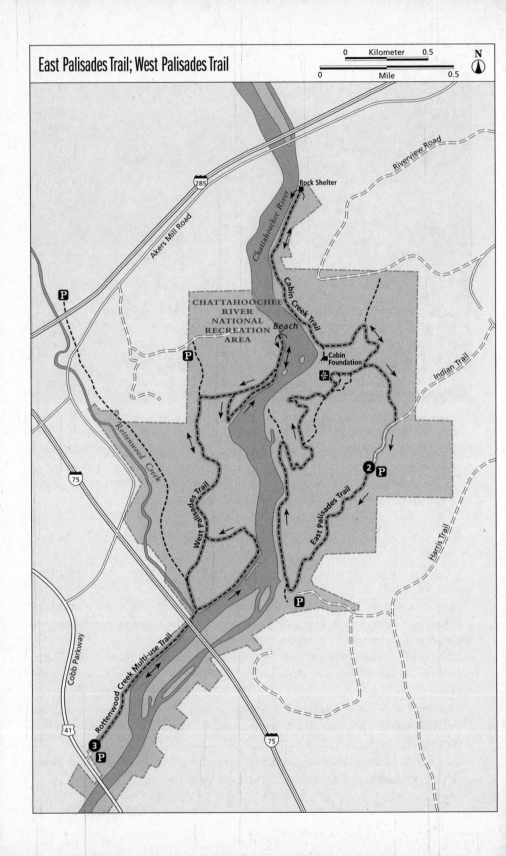

East Palisades Trail; West Palisades Trail

0 Kilometer 0.5

0 Mile 0.5

N

285

Akers Mill Road

Riverview Road

Chattahoochee River

Rock Shelter

CHATTAHOOCHEE
RIVER
NATIONAL
RECREATION
AREA

Beach

Cabin Creek Trail

Cabin
Foundation

Indian Trail

Rottenwood Creek

75

West Palisades Trail

East Palisades Trail

2 P

P

Harris Trail

Cobb Parkway

41

75

3 P

Rottenwood Creek Multi-use Trail

The path crosses a bridge over Cabin Creek and then 100 yards farther enters an old roadbed to follow the stream down to the river. Along the way you pass the junction of a trail on the right that connects to Riverview Road. However, there is no parking at the road on the other end of this trail.

At the mouth of the creek, the stone foundation of a cabin is on the left. The trail now turns upriver across a stone bridge. As it continues, the path next crosses a bridge over Mountain Heath Creek and then runs between a rock cliff on the right and a stand of bamboo on the left. Some of these plants are 5 to 6 inches in diameter.

The trail ends on top of a stone outcrop and rock shelter at the recreation area property boundary. Retrace your path back to the junction with the East Palisades Trail. At the intersection, turn left to reach Indian Trail. A right turn onto that road leads back to the trailhead.

Miles and Directions

0.0 Start from the parking area at the end of Indian Trail.

0.4 After you come down from about 180 feet in elevation to a boardwalk, Long Island Creek is on the left.

0.6 Pass the footbridge leading over Long Island Creek to the alternate trailhead. Begin walking up the Chattahoochee River's east bank.

0.7 Cross the first of several boardwalks over wet areas and continue upstream.

1.0 Cross the bridge over Charlies Trapping Creek.

1.2 The loop trail turns sharply back to the right as you begin an ascent to the overlook. A fisherman's trail runs off to the left at the bend of the pathway, so take care to follow the blazes uphill.

1.3 Reach a trail junction. The trail to the left runs about 150 yards down to the river to a rocky point overlooking Thornton Shoals. This is a one-way trail. Return to the main path and start climbing through several switchbacks.

1.8 Arrive at the top of the bluff with a winter vista of the river. From spring through fall the foliage blocks the view.

2.0 Follow the trail sharply to the left down to the observation deck.

2.1 Reach the deck. Take the trail to the left as you exit the deck to continue.

2.2 Reach the Cabin Creek Trail junction and turn left.

2.3 Cross the first bridge over Cabin Creek.

2.5 Pass the junction with Riverview Road connector trail.

2.6 Cross the second bridge over the creek; reach the river, stone foundation, and stone bridge at the mouth of Cabin Creek. Turn right and walk upstream along the river.

2.7 Cross the bridge over Mountain Heath Creek.

3.1 Reach the rock outcrop and shelter at the turnaround point.

4.0 Arrive back at the junction with the East Palisades Trail. Turn left.

4.3 Turn right onto Indian Trail.

4.6 Reach the trailhead at the parking lot.

3 West Palisades Trail

The West Palisades Unit comprises 302 acres along 1.5 miles of Cochran, Thornton, and Devils Race Course Shoals on the Chattahoochee River. Both the West and East Palisades Units derive their names from the high cliffs along this part of the stream. The trail follows the riverbank and then moves into the rocky palisades uplands. A varied habitat of dense woods, tumbling streams, and rocky cliffs make this area especially interesting.

In sight of Atlanta's skyscraper skyline, you have an almost backwoods-type hiking experience. Cliff-edge views of the Chattahoochee River and stream-edge trails make this a very popular morning or afternoon hike for local residents. Others drive miles just for the experience, which includes wildflowers, birding, fishing for trout, and nature photography.

See map page 18.
Start: At the upstream end of the parking area at the trailhead marker for the Rottenwood Creek Multi-use Trail
Distance: 4.7-mile double-loop lollipop
Hiking time: About 2–2.5 hours
Difficulty: Easy to moderate; one short, steep section
Trail surface: Sandy loam; one portion of old broken pavement
Best season: Year-round
Other trail users: Mountain bikes, anglers
Canine compatibility: Leashed dogs permitted

Land status: Chattahoochee River National Recreation Area (CRNRA)
Nearest town: Smyrna
Fees and permits: Daily parking fee
Schedule: Park opens dawn to dusk, year-round
Maps: USGS Fayetteville; page-size map available from the CRNRA office at Island Ford or online at www.nps.gov/chat
Trail contacts: National Park Service, Chattahoochee River National Recreation Area, 1978 Island Ford Pkwy., Atlanta 30350; (678) 538-1200; www.nps.gov/chat

Finding the trailhead: From exit 19 on I-285, travel south on US 41 (Cobb Parkway) to the Chattahoochee River bridge. Turn right just before the bridge into the Paces Mill Unit of the CRNRA. The trailhead is at the upstream end of the parking area. Trailhead GPS: N33 52.277'/W84 27.215'

The Hike

The trail begins on the west side of the river across from the toe of Long Island. The first portion of the trail shares the path with the paved Rottenwood Creek Multi-use Trail and is wheelchair accessible. Once off the paved portion, the West Palisades Trail is blue blazed, with most of the marks on stakes beside the path.

After you pass under the I-75 bridge, a good vista upstream of the Chattahoochee River is presented, looking toward the bend at the Whitewater Creek Unit of the CRNRA. A footbridge crosses Rottenwood Creek, and the path continues straight,

The deep bend pool at Diving Rock in Sandy Bottom

leaving the paved trail that turns left to follow Rottenwood upstream. Continue upriver, walking under a typical riverbank forest of sycamore, sweet gum, water oak, river birch, ironwood, and box elders. The ridge to the left of the trail supports many wildflowers, including azalea, mountain laurel, dogwoods, trout lilies, trilliums, Solomon's seal, phlox, and violets. Privet shrubs have invaded the riverbank in places, forming dense thickets. Large yellow poplars, loblolly pines, and an occasional decid-uous magnolia are in the coves leading away from the river. In October the hickories, maples, sassafras, dogwoods, sumacs, and red oaks put on a beautiful show of color.

Short spur trails used by fishermen lead to the riverbank. Look for great blue her-ons feeding in the river and for mammal tracks in the moist sandy-clay areas. Belted kingfishers, wood ducks, and Canada geese can be seen regularly along this portion of the trail. Signs of beaver activity are common.

At an intersection marked with a directional stake, the trail turns off to the left. Most of the trail junctions have a map mounted on a post showing where you are. The trail now begins a 0.4-mile climb to the ridge above the river valley. At the next inter-section you have completed half of the first loop; turn right and continue the climb.

Mountain laurel, rhododendron, and several species of ferns dot the passage as you climb to the ridgeline with its chestnut oaks, white oaks, and hickories. It is easy to imagine yourself in the more remote mountains instead of metropolitan Atlanta. The sound of traffic gives way to the murmurs of the river and forest.

The I-75 bridge over the Chattahoochee from the footbridge over Rottenwood Creek

At the point the trail turns sharply to the right, an old paved driveway goes to the left, leaving the park service property. Keep to the right until the trail crosses the headwaters of tiny Trout Lily Creek.

The path then reaches a gravel service road used by park service vehicles only. It follows the bed of the old James Hayes Road, leading steeply downhill toward the river and the area known as Sandy Bottom. A couple of the steepest portions have old, broken concrete pavement. At the bottom of the hill is the intersection at the beginning of the second loop. Turn right to walk it in a counterclockwise direction.

After crossing a footbridge and a boardwalk, the trail turns sharply back upstream along Thornton Shoals. Next is a deep bend of the river with a small boat ramp. On the opposite shore is Diving Rock, where rafters stop in the warmer months to take the 20-foot plunge into the water from an overhanging boulder.

The path next passes the junction at the upper end of the second loop, continuing up an old roadbed to a sandy beach at the foot of Devils Race Course Shoals. From the beach, retrace your path back to the loop intersection and turn right past a building containing restrooms. These are provided for rafters and canoeists on the river.

The next junction closes the second loop; turn right and climb back up the service road to where the trail exits to the left. Continue to retrace your earlier path back to the intersection at the first loop. Turn right and follow the very rutted trail downhill to its junction with the Rottenwood Multi-Use Trail. Turn left and follow the paved path back to the trailhead.

Miles and Directions

0.0   Start from the parking lot along the Rottenwood Creek Multi-use Trail.

0.6   Pass under the I-75 bridge, over the footbridge across Rottenwood Creek, and continue straight, leaving the paved path.

1.0   Turn left at the intersection, climbing away from the river.

1.2   Turn to the right at this intersection, ending half of the first loop.

1.7   Pass the old paved drive leading to the left out of the park. Stay to the right.

1.8   Cross Trout Lily Creek.

1.9   Turn right onto the service road, walking downhill to the river.

2.1   Reach the intersection for the second loop and turn right.

2.2   Cross the footbridge.

2.3   Cross a boardwalk and turn sharply upstream along Thornton Shoals.

2.4   Pass the boat ramp and view of Diving Rock.

2.5   Reach the other end of the second loop; continue straight on the old roadbed.

2.7   Turn around at the beach at Devils Race Course.

2.8   Turn right at the intersection and pass the restrooms.

2.9   Close the second loop and turn right up the service road.

3.1   Turn left off the service road.

3.8   At the intersection on the first loop, turn right.

4.1   Turn left on the paved Rottenwood Creek Multi-use Trail.

4.7   Arrive back at the trailhead and parking area.

4 Johnson Ferry North Trail

The Johnson Ferry Unit of the Chattahoochee River National Recreation Area (CRNRA) comprises 108 acres entirely on the floodplain of the Chattahoochee River. This unit also provides a picnic area, along with boat ramp and launch area for canoes and rafts on the river.

The trail is on the west side of the river upstream from Johnson Ferry Road. This is an exceptionally good birding area with aquatic, open, brushy, and forested habitats. Ducks, herons, beavers, muskrats, raccoons, opossums, otters, turtles, frogs, and toads are some of the wildlife associated with the wet area and river. The forested area attracts many songbirds. Several benches are positioned along the riverside portion of the trail for wildlife viewing.

A single-loop, blue-blazed trail takes you around the unique and extensive wetland area with several creek crossings. For half the distance you are in almost constant view of the river. After the turn along the banks of Mulberry Creek, the return is via a very straight walk through brushy cover and larger trees.

Start: The path begins at a trailhead sign, gate, and large rock at the north end of the parking area.
Distance: 1.7-mile loop
Hiking time: About 1 hour
Difficulty: Easy
Trail surface: Sandy loam; short gravel section
Best season: Year-round
Other trail users: Hikers only
Canine compatibility: Leashed dogs permitted
Land status: Chattahoochee River National Recreation Area

Nearest town: Sandy Springs
Fees and permits: Daily parking fee
Schedule: Unit open dawn to dusk, year-round
Maps: USGS Sandy Springs; page-size map available from the park service office at Island Ford or from www.nps.gov/chat
Trail contacts: National Park Service, Chattahoochee River National Recreation Area, 1978 Island Ford Pkwy., Atlanta 30350; (678) 538-1200; www.nps.gov/chat

Finding the trailhead: From I-285 take exit 25 (Roswell Road) and go north on Roswell Road 1.7 miles to Johnson Ferry Road. Turn left and go 2.2 miles and cross the Chattahoochee River Bridge. Immediately across the bridge, turn right at the sign for the Johnson Ferry North parking area. Follow the gravel road through the gate to the boat ramp and parking area. Trailhead GPS: N33 56.806'/W84 24.220'

The Hike

This trail is an easy but interesting path that goes around a natural wetland area. From the trailhead at the parking area, walk past the information sign, gate, and large rock onto an old gravel roadbed. This is to the right of the return loop of the trail, which is also on an old gravel road.

The first part of the trail is on an old gravel roadbed.

During spring and summer, you may see killdeers in the gravel and grassy areas.

Roughly 200 yards into the hike, the path merges with the return loop as they both cross a culvert over Nannyberry Creek. From there the trail turns right and approaches the riverbank.

Spur trails made by fishermen lead off the main path at irregular intervals. During periods when the water in the river is very clear or low, it is possible to see a dark V-shaped area crossing the channel. This is the remains of a fish trap used by early settlers. It is believed that white settlers learned to build and use fish traps from the Indians.

Privet shrubs and switch cane grow in dense thickets along the trail close to the river. The privet is an escaped horticultural plant. The cane is native and in the past extended in great patches along many of the rivers of the Southeast. The large canebrakes of the past were used extensively by both wildlife and humans.

The first half of the loop offers many views of the Chattahoochee River.

After crossing a cleared gas line right-of-way and continuing past a bench, the trail reaches a sign marking River Mile 311 in the edge of the water. These miles are measured from the Woodruff Dam on Lake Seminole in southwest Georgia, where the Chattahoochee and Flint Rivers join to form the Apalachicola River.

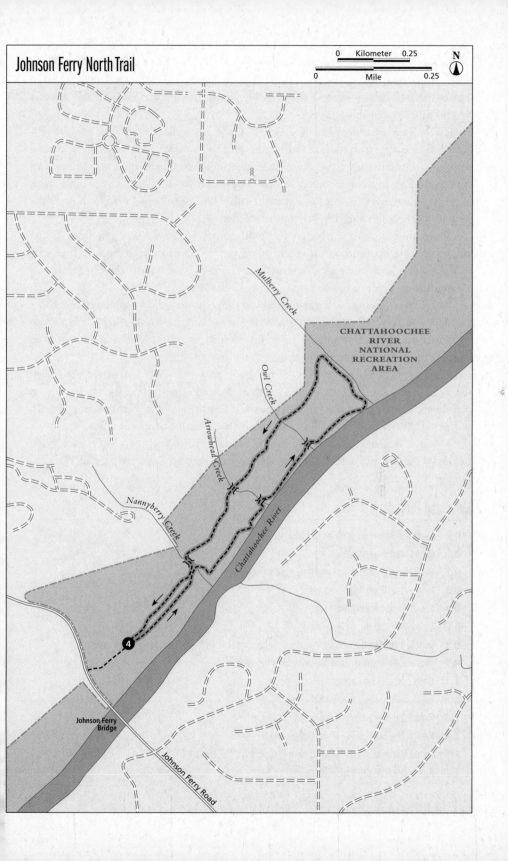

Johnson Ferry North Trail

0 Kilometer 0.25
0 Mile 0.25

N

Mulberry Creek

CHATTAHOOCHEE
RIVER
NATIONAL
RECREATION
AREA

Owl Creek

Arrowhead Creek

Nannyberry Creek

Chattahoochee River

4

Johnson Ferry
Bridge

Johnson Ferry Road

Beyond the river marker the trail turns left to cross a culvert over Arrowhead Creek. It then returns to the river shore. Two more benches along the bank are passed before the trail crosses over Owl Creek on yet another culvert. There's also another bench just north of this crossing.

Just before reaching Mulberry Creek, the main trail turns to the left. A well-beaten fisherman's path continues ahead toward the mouth of the creek, so be careful to follow the blue blazes. As you walk along Mulberry Creek, the area is alive with yellow jonquils in the late winter months. A pipe crosses the creek to the right, with another well-worn path continuing at the other end of the pipe. That trail leaves the park property, following the river upstream.

Continuing toward the ridge, the path comes to a four-way junction. A trail continues straight ahead up the creek valley, and another fords the creek to the right. Both of those leave the park property. Turn sharply left to follow the blue blazes on the trail along the foot of the ridge.

You are now hiking back downstream on the opposite side of a wet, and sometimes flooded, area. Watch for cardinals, yellow-breasted chats, brown thrashers, catbirds, and mockingbirds. The ridge side of the trail is rich in ferns and hosts wildflowers from early spring to early winter.

After stepping across tiny Owl Creek, you pass a connector trail entering from the right and then cross the bridge over Arrowhead Creek. Next the trail reaches a boardwalk that turns to the left and ends at a footbridge over a small water flow. In the woods to the right are what appear to be the remains of an old stable.

The trail next merges with the outbound loop to recross the culvert over Nannyberry Creek. Once across, take the fork to the right for the walk back to close the loop at the trailhead.

Miles and Directions

0.0   Pass the sign and gate at the trailhead.

0.1   Cross Nannyberry Creek.

0.2   Pass through a cleared gas line right-of-way.

0.3   Reach the River Mile 311 sign.

0.4   Cross Arrowhead Creek.

0.6   Cross Owl Creek.

0.8   Turn left up Mulberry Creek and pass the junction with the trail across the pipe.

0.9   Reach the four-way trail junction and turn left.

1.1   Step across Owl Creek.

1.2   Pass the connector trail to the right.

1.3   Cross the bridge over Arrowhead Creek.

1.4   Reach the boardwalk and bridge.

1.5   Cross Nannyberry Creek and take the right fork of the trail.

1.7   Arrive back at the trailhead.

Honorable Mention

A Chattahoochee River National Recreation Area: Cochran Shoals Unit Trails

The Cochran Shoals Unit comprises 968 acres, the largest and most popular park along the Chattahoochee River National Recreation Area (CRNRA). There are fields, woodlands, wetlands, and river habitats. This is a good birding and wildlife-watching trail.

Ten miles of interconnected trails offer a variety of natural and historic attractions. Most of the trail system is on jogging, fitness, and bike trails. The wheelchair-accessible fitness trail is a 2.5-mile loop that follows close to the river. Two other trails, about 1.5 miles each, lead away from the heavily used areas into forested hiking paths. The degree of difficulty varies from easy to moderate. The ruins of the old Marietta Paper Mill add historic interest to the area.

The Cochran Shoals area is located close to major office and residential areas of Atlanta, and hundreds of hikers, bikers, joggers, and others use it daily. All trails can be reached on foot from three parking areas on the west side of the river. The unit is accessible year-round.

This area is just north of the I-285 bridge across the Chattahoochee River. A page-size map is available from the park service office.

For more information: National Park Service, Chattahoochee River National Recreation Area, 1978 Island Ford Pkwy., Atlanta 30350; (678) 538-1200; www.nps .gov/chat

DeLorme: Georgia Atlas and Gazetteer: Page 20 H2

5 Kennesaw Mountain National Battlefield Park Trails

Kennesaw Mountain National Battlefield Park covers 2,923 acres of rolling hills just northwest of Atlanta. From June 19 to July 2, 1864, it was the site of a bloody Civil War battle between the Confederate Army of Tennessee under Gen. Joseph E. Johnston and the Union Army of the Tennessee commanded by Gen. William T. Sherman.

Reminders of those days of conflict are visible throughout the park and dictate land use today. More than 8 miles of trenches, rifle pits, and other earthworks in the Cheatham Hill region are some of the best preserved from the period.

Kennesaw Mountain rises abruptly 1,000 feet above the surrounding Piedmont Plateau to the southeast and the Ridge and Valley area to the northwest. Along with neighboring Little Kennesaw Mountain and Pigeon Hill, the three heights add changes of elevation to the park's hikes.

The trail system features 15.8 miles of paths and is considered one of the nation's best urban hiking destinations. All of the hikes, however, are day treks. No camping is allowed.

There are more than twenty officially named paths, but combinations of these can be broken down into five longer options.

The 9.5-mile West Trail runs from the visitor center to Kolb Farm Trail. The East Trail connects those same two points and is 7.4 miles in length. The Visitor Center to Pigeon Hill, Cheatham Hill to Kolb Farm, and Burnt Hickory to Cheatham Hill Loops all are composed of portions of the East and West Trails.

The featured trail is the Visitor Center to Pigeon Hill Loop, a 5.7-mile trail covering the northern end of the park.

Start: At the visitor center and museum
Distance: 5.7-mile loop
Hiking time: About 2 hours
Difficulty: Easy to moderate, with short strenuous stretches on the mountainsides
Trail surface: Hard-packed dirt, with some paved and gravel stretches
Best season: Year-round
Other trail users: Joggers
Canine compatibility: Leashed dogs permitted
Land status: National Park Service
Nearest towns: Marietta

Fees and permits: None
Schedule: Park hours, dawn to dusk, year-round
Maps: USGS Marietta; hiking trail map available online at www.nps.gov/kemo/planyourvisit/maps.htm
Trail contacts: Kennesaw Mountain National Battlefield Park, 900 Kennesaw Mountain Dr., Kennesaw 30152; (770) 427-4686 Ext. 0; www.nps.gov/kemo/index.htm; Kennesaw Mountain Trail Club; www.kennesawmountaintrailclub.org.

Finding the trailhead: For the Visitor Center to Pigeon Hill Loop, from exit 269 on I-75, go west on Barrett Parkway for approximately 3 miles. Turn left onto Old US 41 and go 1.4 miles to the intersection with Stilesboro Road. Turn right and the visitor center is immediately on the left. Trailhead GPS: N33 58.946'/W84 34.680'

The Hike

From the trailhead at the visitor center, begin climbing steadily up the face of Kennesaw Mountain on the Kennesaw Mountain Trail. Halfway up, the trail merges into an old road running across the mountainside. Soon the path leaves the old road, turning uphill to the right. At this point it passes through a rock formation that offers an overlook of the town of Marietta.

Switching back up the mountain, the trail passes another outcrop with a bench for resting. Along this north face of the mountain, the forest is dominated by chestnut oak trees. Virginia creepers are present in the rocky areas.

As you reach the parking lot near the mountain crest, a stone overlook provides a great view of the Atlanta skyline to the southeast. A paved walkway now leads up to the peak of the mountain.

Along the way the path passes three of the vintage cannons in their earthworks pointing to the north. On top of the mountain the trail splits into a short paved loop running around the crest.

Sweeping views are available of Atlanta to the southeast and the Allatoona Mountains to the northwest. Some of the rocks bear very old carvings left by early tourists. Such actions are illegal today.

The paved trail ends at the fourth cannon, with the path reverting to packed dirt as it continues down the steep back slope. Where the trail crosses Kennesaw Mountain Drive coming up the mountain, a panorama of Little Kennesaw's crest appears. This also is the end of the Kennesaw Mountain Trail and the beginning of the Little Kennesaw Mountain Trail.

Walking through the swell between the mountains, continue up a gentle slope to a very large flat rock near the top of Little Kennesaw. Here you see prickly pear and lamb's ear growing along the trail. At the peak of Little Kennesaw, the four additional cannons of Fort McBride face the north of the mountain.

The descent down the back side of Little Kennesaw is quite steep, rocky, and uneven. It passes a number of red cedar trees as the trail switches back and forth down the slope, going through one extremely large rock outcrop.

Finally the path levels out on top of Pigeon Hill, reaching the junction with a shortcut trail on the left running to the Camp Brumby Trail. Go straight on the path that now becomes the Pigeon Hill Loop. The trail runs amid Confederate rifle pits, large boulders, and twisted trees on the crest of Pigeon Hill.

As the pathway drops off Pigeon Hill, it crosses an area of exposed rocks with more prickly pear and bear grass. At the next junction, turn sharply left onto the Pigeon Hill Cut-off. The Pigeon Hill Loop continues straight down the slope as part of the Burnt Hickory to Cheatham Hill Loop Trail.

The trail soon passes another intersection with the Burnt Hickory to Cheatham Hill Loop going to the right. Turn to the left onto the Camp Brumby Trail on an old road and quickly pass the other end of the shortcut trail from Pigeon Hill. The hike

A series of four cannons sits along the path at the top of Kennesaw Mountain.

then passes through a long stretch of oak, hickory, and pine forest. At one point the right side of the trail consists of board fences at the back of a neighborhood.

Also before you leave this old road, grassy clearings appear on the left at the site of the ruins of the Civilian Conservation Corps's Camp Brumby, dating from the 1930s when the park was first developed.

After exiting the old road to the left, the path passes the junction with the Camp Brumby Cut-off Link. The trail to the right runs to Kennesaw Avenue and Marietta. Turn left onto the Cut-off Link. Upon entering a large grassy field, the path skirts the left side of the opening as it follows the foot of the mountain back to the visitor center and trailhead.

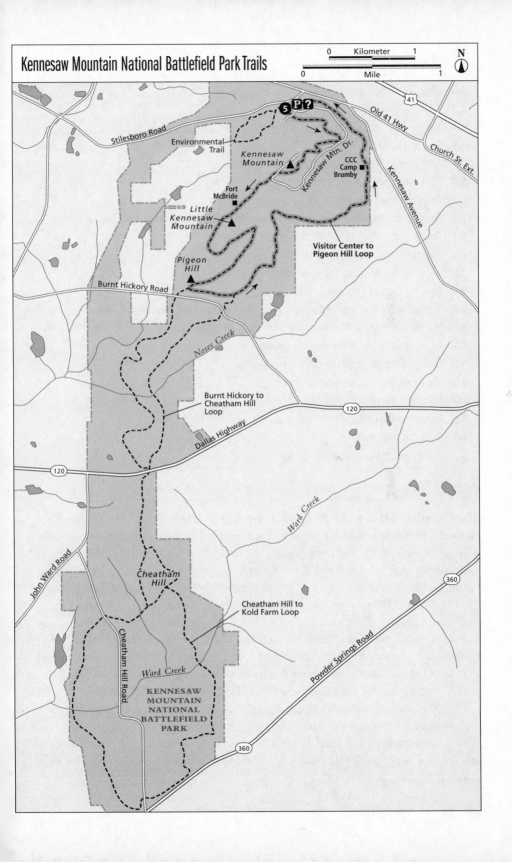

Kennesaw Mountain National Battlefield Park Trails

0 Kilometer 1

0 Mile 1

N

Stilesboro Road

Old 41 Hwy

41

Church St. Ext.

Environmental Trail

Kennesaw Mountain

Kennesaw Mtn. Dr.

CCC Camp Brumby

Kennesaw Avenue

Fort McBride

Little Kennesaw Mountain

Visitor Center to Pigeon Hill Loop

Pigeon Hill

Burnt Hickory Road

Noses Creek

Burnt Hickory to Cheatham Hill Loop

120

Dallas Highway

120

Ward Creek

John Ward Road

Cheatham Hill

Cheatham Hill to Kold Farm Loop

360

Cheatham Hill Road

Ward Creek

KENNESAW MOUNTAIN NATIONAL BATTLEFIELD PARK

Powder Springs Road

360

Miles and Directions

0.0 Begin climbing the mountain from the visitor center.

0.2 Enter the old roadbed.

0.4 Exit the road at the rock outcrop and Marietta overlook.

0.6 Pass the second rock outcrop.

0.8 Skirt the mountaintop parking area.

1.0 Reach the crest of Kennesaw Mountain.

1.2 Cross the paved drive between the mountains.

1.6 The large flat rock straddles the trail on Little Kennesaw Mountain.

1.7 Pass Fort McBride at the mountain peak.

2.1 Traverse a very large rock outcrop.

2.5 The shortcut connector trail is on the left.

2.6 Pass the crest of Pigeon Hill.

2.8 Turn left at the trail intersection to continue on the Visitor Center to Pigeon Hill Loop.

3.2 The Burnt Hickory to Cheatham Hill Loop splits off to the right.

3.3 Pass the other end of the shortcut trail on the left.

4.2 Backyard neighborhood fences are on the right.

4.8 The Camp Brumby ruins are on the left.

5.0 Go left off the old roadbed.

5.1 Turn left at the junction with the Camp Brumby Cut-off Link.

5.5 Enter the open field.

5.7 Arrive back at the trailhead.

Options

The **Cheatham Hill to Kolb Farm Loop** trail usually is walked from the parking area on Cheatham Hill Road. This trail traverses the southern portion of the park where the preliminary Battle of Kolb Farm took place on June 22, 1864, between Confederate Gen. John Bell Hood and Union Gen. Joseph Hooker. The historic Kolb farmhouse lies just across Powder Springs Road from the trail's southernmost point.

The **Burnt Hickory to Cheatham Hill Loop** trail connects the Visitor Center to Pigeon Hill and Cheatham Hill to Kolb Farm Loops. It can be walked as a 6.0-mile figure eight, with small loops on each end. The southern end of the hike is along Confederate earthworks with interspersed cannons. The northern portion has more hills, with several creek crossings. It features the sites of the Hardage Sawmill, New Salem Baptist Church, and Confederate Gen. Leonidas Polk's headquarters.

The trail also can be used as a connector with the other two loop trails to create a 15.8-mile hike through the park.

The **Environmental Trail** offers a 1.3-mile walk featuring the natural history and habitats of the park. The trailhead is at the visitor center's picnic area. This path does not connect with the other park hikes.

6 Sweetwater Creek State Park Trails

Sweetwater Creek State Park has a wilderness feel, offering many species of wildflowers and wildlife, a beautiful forest, and cascading Sweetwater Creek—all only minutes from downtown Atlanta. Sweetwater Creek is a fast-flowing stream that winds its way through a granite-boulder streambed in a well-protected wooded valley.

During the Civil War, cloth was manufactured at the New Manchester Manufacturing Company for Confederate troops. This proved the factory's undoing. Gen. William T. Sherman ordered the factory and town to be burned on July 9, 1864. The mostly women and children working at the mill were told to pack for a long trip, loaded into wagons, and eventually placed in a prison camp in Louisville, Kentucky. The town of New Manchester never was rebuilt.

The 2,549-acre park features picnicking, as well as boating and fishing on 215-acre George H. Sparks Reservoir. There also are 9 miles of hiking trails within the park.

The Red/History Trail offers a walk through old New Manchester down to Sweetwater Falls. The Blue Trail provides an alternate access to the falls on the overlooking ridges. The Yellow Trail crosses the creek onto the opposite ridges, and the White Trail runs through woodlands and fields from the interpretive center to the waterfall.

The featured trail is a loop combining the Red/History and White Trails.

Start: At the parking area near the interpretive center
Distance: 3.9-mile loop
Hiking time: About 1.5–2 hours
Difficulty: Mostly easy to moderate; a few strenuous sections
Trail surface: Clay loam, with rocky and gravel sections
Best season: Year-round
Other trail users: Hikers, joggers
Canine compatibility: Leashed dogs permitted

Land status: Georgia DNR, State Parks & Historic Sites Division
Nearest town: Lithia Springs
Fees and permits: Daily parking fee
Schedule: Park hours 7 a.m.–sunset, year-round
Maps: USGS Austell, Campbellton, Mableton, and Ben Hill; trail map available from the park office
Trail contacts: Sweetwater Creek State Park, 1750 Mount Vernon Rd., Lithia Springs 30122; (770) 732-5871; www.gastateparks.org

Finding the trailhead: From Atlanta take I-20 West to exit 44 at Thornton Road. Turn left and go 0.4 mile to Blairs Bridge Road. Turn right and go 2.1 miles to Mt. Vernon Road. Turn left and go 1.3 miles to the park entrance on the left. Go 0.7 mile on Factory Shoals Road to the interpretive center and parking area. The parking area is the trailhead for all trails. Trailhead GPS: N33 45.206'/W84 37.685'

The Hike

The park's trails are well blazed and are interpreted in a leaflet, available at the park office. Numbered markers correspond to the interpretive leaflet. More than 120

The ruins of the New Manchester Mill are the focal point on the Red/History Trail.

wildflowers bloom along the trails in the park from early February to mid-June. There is a large wooden trail map at the trailhead.

A tree-covered gravel walkway leaves the parking area, carrying the Red/History Trail under a canopy of a dozen species of trees. The trail descends the ridge down to Sweetwater Creek, passing the junction with the Yellow Trail on the left.

At the creek the path turns downstream to the right. Through here the creek and valley are just as fascinating as the trail's historical features. The trail quickly reaches the head of the old millrace, which forms a narrow canal between the path and creek. A footbridge crosses the race to a parallel path running downstream on the narrow island to the left. Look for native azaleas and mountain laurels.

After you cross a footbridge, the Blue Trail intersects from the right. Turning onto it takes you back to the parking lot.

The New Manchester Mill ruins now appear on the left on the creek shore. A couple of observation decks are available for viewing the structure. The Blue Trail also runs off to the right and downstream along the ridge side at this point.

The Red/History Trail descends left down several flights of wooden steps to the creek shore. This path now follows the creek right at the water. Along the way it climbs over one rock protrusion that has a cable handrail to permit safe passage. The granite cliffs along the bank and the cascades on the stream are spectacular through

Sweetwater Falls draws both hikers and kayakers to Sweetwater Creek.

here. The rock cliffs support many interesting plants, such as rockcap fern, liverworts, and mosses.

After crossing a wooden footbridge, the trail climbs thirty-nine steps built into the hillside, leading up to an observation deck. Another 0.3 mile along the trail is the overlook for Sweetwater Falls. This drop and slide are favorites with kayakers on the stream.

The Red/History Trail ends here, at the junction with the Blue and White Trails. The Blue Trail runs uphill to the right, while the White Trail continues downstream along the creek. Quickly the path descends seventy-three wooden steps to get back down to water level.

Continue along the creek to the mouth of Jacks Branch. The trail runs up the valley along this tumbling brook flowing over gravel and granite. Large chain ferns, cinnamon ferns, Christmas ferns, and other moist-soil plants are abundant along the branch. Be aware there is a bridge over Jacks Branch near its mouth that carries a foot trail farther downstream. This path is not part of the park's regular trail system and is not connected to the other trails at any other point.

Climbing steadily up the side of the ridge, the path crosses a footbridge and then reaches the dam on Jacks Lake, a long, narrow pond frequented by beavers, turtles, wood ducks, and herons.

The trail next skirts the lake on an unpaved road overlooking the water. The trail remains on this old road for most of the rest of the hike.

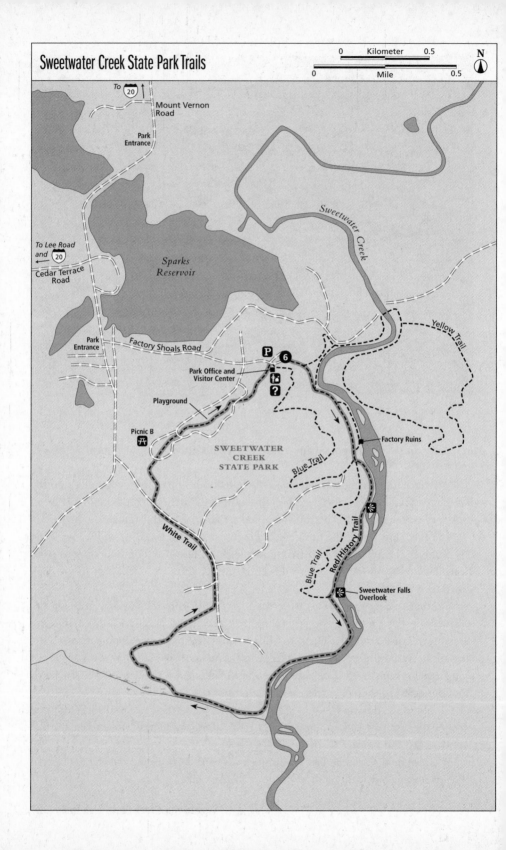

Sweetwater Creek State Park Trails

0 Kilometer 0.5
0 Mile 0.5

N

To 20

Mount Vernon Road

Park Entrance

To Lee Road and 20

Cedar Terrace Road

Sparks Reservoir

Sweetwater Creek

Park Entrance

Factory Shoals Road

Yellow Trail

P 6

Park Office and Visitor Center

Playground

Picnic B

SWEETWATER CREEK STATE PARK

Blue Trail

Factory Ruins

White Trail

Blue Trail

Red/History Trail

Sweetwater Falls Overlook

The unpaved road leads through a forest and into open fields known as the Jacks Hill Area. The field edges with young trees like persimmon, sumac, loblolly pine, and oaks add an interesting diversion from the more mature forest. Several service roads are crossed or branch off the trail. It is necessary to keep the white blazes in sight.

Along the way the hike passes the foundation of an old home place on the right. This region is ablaze in yellow in the early spring when the massive beds of jonquils are blooming.

After going through pine stands and some hardwoods, the trail crosses two paved drives in the picnic and playground area before reaching the parking area and trailhead.

Miles and Directions

0.0　Start downhill toward the creek from the trailhead and parking area.

0.1　Pass the Yellow Trail on left, reach the creek shore, and turn right.

0.3　Reach the head of the millrace and bridge across the race on the left.

0.5　Cross a footbridge and come to the intersection with the Blue Trail and the observation decks for the factory ruins.

0.6　The Blue Trail splits off to the right, and the Red/History Trail goes left down the wooden stairs to the creek bank.

0.7　Pass the rock protrusion with cable handrail.

0.8　Cross the footbridge and climb the steps to the observation deck.

1.0　Reach the end of the Red/History Trail at the Sweetwater Falls Overlook. Continue downstream on the White Trail.

1.1　Climb down the seventy-three steps to the creek bank.

1.7　Make a 90-degree right turn, leaving Sweetwater Creek to go up Jacks Branch.

1.9　Cross a footbridge and reach the dam on Jacks Lake.

2.5　After a long climb, reach the first wildlife clearing in the Jacks Hill Area.

2.7　Pass the old home foundation on the right.

3.4　Cross a paved park drive and enter the picnic and playground area.

3.7　Cross a second paved park drive.

3.9　Arrive back at the parking area to close the loop at the trailhead.

Options

The 2.0-mile **Blue Trail** intersects the Red/History Trail at two points near the mill ruins and again at Sweetwater Falls. It can be combined with the Red/History hike to create a 3.0-mile loop covering the creek bank and the ridges above. This trail begins in the interpretive center parking lot, a few yards south of the main trailhead.

The **Yellow Trail** is not associated with the historical significance of Sweetwater Creek; rather it forms a 3.0-mile lollipop from the common trailhead and offers a more nature-oriented hike. After splitting off the Red/History Trail, the path crosses the Army Bridge over Sweetwater Creek. The trail then circles an upland ridgetop on the eastern side of the creek.

7 Panola Mountain State Park Trails

The centerpiece of the park is the granite dome of Panola Mountain. The mountain rises to 940 feet of elevation, but that is only 260 feet above the South River, which flows along its northern edge.

Of the several similar domes in the vicinity, Panola is the only one left undisturbed. Unique granite outcrops and endemic plants and animals are associated with this peculiar habitat. The 1,635-acre facility borders a rapidly growing residential area and provides excellent educational outdoor activities for its neighbors. The park's nature center has excellent displays of local geology, plants, and wildlife, while park personnel offer frequent nature walks for children and adults.

Three trails totaling 4.9 miles offer interpretive walks through this unique habitat. The Rock Outcrop, Watershed, and Panola Mountain Trails provide information on the area's geology, fauna, flora, and history. The Fitness and 3-D Target Trails also are in the park.

The park also is tied to the nearby Davidson–Arabia Mountain Nature Preserve and the town of Lithonia by the paved, 12-mile, 10-foot-wide multiuse Arabia Mountain Trail.

The featured hike is a double loop composed of the Watershed and Rock Outcrop Trails.

Start: At the rear of the nature center
Distance: 1.4-mile double loop
Hiking time: About 1 hour
Difficulty: Easy
Trail surface: Dirt and gravel
Best season: Year-round
Other trail users: Hikers only
Canine compatibility: No dogs permitted
Land status: Georgia DNR, State Parks & Historic Sites Division

Nearest towns: Lithonia, Stockbridge
Fees and permits: Daily parking fee
Schedule: Park hours, 7 a.m.–dusk, year-round
Maps: USGS Redan and Stockbridge; page-size map of the park available at the park nature center
Trail contacts: Panola Mountain State Park, 2600 SR 155 Southwest, Stockbridge 30281; (770) 389-7801; www.gastateparks.org

Finding the trailhead: From exit 68 on I-20, take Wesley Chapel Road south for 0.3 mile to Snapfinger Road. Turn left and go 1.8 miles. At this point the road picks up SR 155; continue straight for 5 miles more. The entrance for Panola Mountain State Park is on the left. All trails share the same trailhead at the nature center. Trailhead GPS: N33 37.575'/W84 10.300'

The Hike

Combining the 0.9-mile Watershed and 0.5-mile Rock Outcrop Trails creates a double-loop hike that takes you through the major habitat types in the park. The paths are best walked in a counterclockwise direction beginning with the Watershed Trail.

The authors examine a large boulder that has a split, called a joint, running its length.

On either trail wildlife such as deer, squirrels, rabbits, raccoons, opossums, skunks, and chipmunks may be seen, along with lizards and other reptiles. Butterflies abound during the summer months, feeding on the wide variety of flowering plants.

The red-blazed Watershed Trail leads off to the right behind the nature center and passes through a mixed pine-hardwood forest with undergrowth of sweet gum, sassafras, maple, yellow poplar, and dogwood, along with honeysuckle and muscadine vines. Strawberry bush is common, with its strikingly colorful fruits in fall. Ferns are abundant and include bracken, Christmas, wood, and cinnamon varieties, as well as brown-stemmed spleenwort. Also look for the blue blossoms of elephant's-foot in the spring. The plant's leaves grow flat to the ground.

Climb a set of stone steps at the point a connector trail from the parking lot enters from the right and continue to the left. At the next junction where the loop portion of the Watershed Trail starts, turn right.

Quickly a fence appears on the right of the trail beside a deep erosion gully. This is the first of many such reminders of past farming activities on the land. Next the trail forks, just before crossing a footbridge. The left fork leads about 40 yards to an observation deck affording a good perspective of the deepness of the eroded ravines.

Returning to the fork, turn left across the bridge and continue downhill. After crossing a bridge over another gully, the path reaches a small creek bottom. Here the forest is almost completely hardwoods with large sweet gums, yellow poplars, beeches, several species of oaks, and an occasional large loblolly pine.

The authors overlook the exposed granite from the observation deck.

The path crosses the stream twice on footbridges, with another observation deck between them. Large patches of New York ferns grow in the moist alluvial soil along the creek.

The trail then begins to gain elevation, passing another observation deck on the right before closing the loop. At this point, turn right and walk back to the trailhead.

At the trailhead, turn right onto the white-blazed Rock Outcrop Trail and immediately pass the junction with the Panola Mountain Trail leading off to the right. At the next intersection, a shortcut connector trail leads to the left.

The path now passes through boulder-strewn woods leading to an observation deck over the large exposed sheet of granite. Just before reaching the open rock, there is a large boulder on the left that has a fissure running completely through it.

During late summer and fall, masses of yellow flowers, locally known as Confederate daisies and found only on and around these granite domes, add spectacular color to the otherwise gray rock outcrops. Other plants around the rocks are sparkleberry, American beauty berry, and common ragwort. The last also has a yellow flower in spring.

Farther along the path another overlook station offers a grand view of Stone Mountain to the north. From there the trail passes the other end of the shortcut and loops back to the trailhead.

Miles and Directions

0.0 Start downhill to the right on the red-blazed Watershed Trail.

0.1 Pass the junction with the parking lot connector.

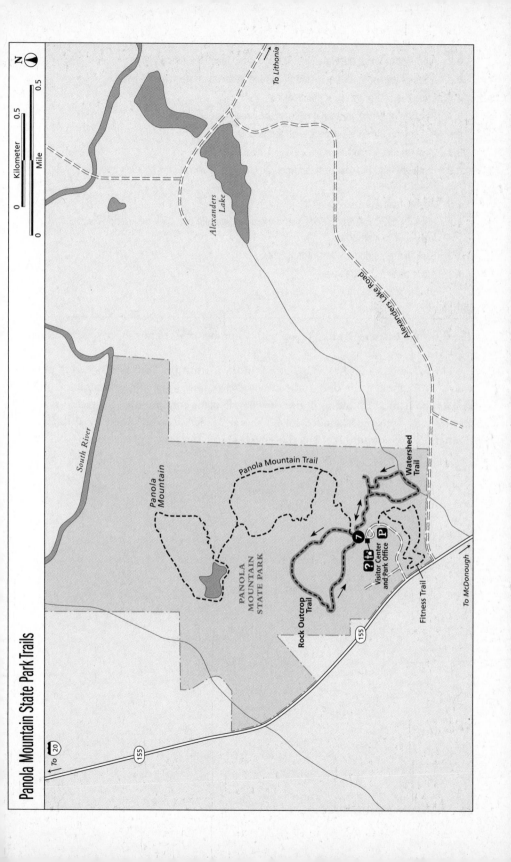

Panola Mountain State Park Trails

0.2 Turn right to begin the Watershed Trail loop and reach the fenced gully.

0.3 Arrive at the footbridge and side trail to the observation deck on the left.

0.4 Cross the first bridge over the creek.

0.5 Pass the observation deck and cross the second creek bridge.

0.6 The upland observation deck is on the right.

0.7 Close the loop and turn right.

0.9 Turn right onto the white-blazed Rock Outcrop Trail and pass the junction with the Panola Mountain Trail.

1.0 The shortcut trail runs to the left.

1.2 Arrive at the observation deck over the exposed granite and then the overlook with Stone Mountain to the north.

1.3 Pass the other end of the shortcut trail.

1.4 Arrive back at the trailhead.

Options

The 1.0-mile **Fitness Trail** is a loop with a number of exercise devices placed along it course.

The 3.5-mile, double-loop lollipop **Panola Mountain Trail** is designed to provide a closer look at the undisturbed 100-acre granite dome atop the mountain. To protect the natural condition of the very fragile plant communities, the trail is available only as a scheduled guided hike. The staff leaders interpret the special features throughout the 3-hour hike. Call (800) 864-7275 to arrange a guided hike.

8 Davidson–Arabia Mountain Nature Preserve Trails

Davidson–Arabia Mountain Nature Preserve encompasses 2,550 acres and another of the prominent rock outcrops called monadnocks—isolated hills standing above the surrounding area. These rock outcrops host a unique environment with a wide variety of microhabitats that support a number of endemic plant and animal species.

Arabia Mountain is said to be one hundred million years older than its two local granite-dome cousins—Panola and Stone Mountains. Arabia is noted for the swirling tidal gray rock pattern characteristic of Lithonia gneiss, formed when the mountain's original gneiss was partially melted to form a rock that incorporates both igneous and metamorphic features in a granite-gneiss.

The history of human settlement in this region is intimately connected to its geological resources, starting more than 7,000 years ago with the quarrying and trading of soapstone. Included in the park is the former rock quarry donated by the Davidson family, who operated it until 1972.

Arabia Mountain is home to two federally protected species (black-spored quillwort and pool sprite) as well as several other rare plants unique to the granite-outcrop environment, such as Georgia oaks and the brilliant red diamorpha, which is also known as Small's stonecrop.

Other plants you can expect to find here are sunnybells, sparkleberry, and fringe tree. Mosses and lichens are well adapted to the harsh rock outcrop as well. A plant endemic to these mountains that is quite noticeable is the yellow daisy-like flower called the Confederate daisy that blooms in masses in late summer.

There are eight hiking trails in the preserve, as well as a portion of the long multiuse Arabia Mountain Trail. These trails have been designed to expose you to as many of the different habitats as possible and the history of the area.

The featured hike combines the 1.2-mile Forest and 1.0-mile Mile Rock Trails to create a loop beginning and ending at the Davidson–Arabia Mountain Nature Center.

Start: At the information sign beside the nature center
Distance: 2.4-mile loop
Hiking time: About 1 hour
Difficulty: Easy
Trail surface: Dirt and sandy loam; natural, uneven granite and exposed quarry stone
Best season: Mar–June; Oct–Dec
Other trail users: Hikers only
Canine compatibility: Leashed dogs permitted
Land status: DeKalb County, Natural Resources Management Office
Nearest towns: Lithonia, Conyers

Fees and permits: None
Schedule: Preserve hours 7 a.m.–dusk, year-round
Maps: USGS Conyers and Redan; map of Davidson-Arabia Mountain Nature Preserve available at nature center; Arabia Mountain Trail map available from the PATH Foundation at http://pathfoundation.org/trails/arabia-mountain/
Trail contacts: Davidson-Arabia Mountain Nature Preserve, 3787 Klondike Rd., Lithonia 30038; (770) 492-5220; www.co.dekalb.ga.us/naturalresources/wonders.html

The Hike

The yellow-blazed Forest Trail begins at the Davidson–Arabia Mountain Nature Center information sign, crosses a short boardwalk, and goes through a pleasant pine-hardwood forest to Arabia Lake. You go to the right of and parallel to the wide, paved multiuse Arabia Mountain Trail, crossing it at 0.2 mile to continue on toward the lake.

The most impressive forest feature here is the thickness of the undergrowth and the large loblolly pines. You continue northwest on a soft pine needle and leaf loam trail, passing through an area of large, old, gnarled pines showing the scars of past fires that were common 70 years ago. Openings in the undergrowth give you views of small areas of exposed granite, lined with trees and supporting patches of moss and lichens, along with bunches of flowering plants.

The trail next goes down a few feet to parallel a little intermittent creek. The path eventually crosses the small streambed, where water may puddle up in the trail during wet weather. Just beyond the crossing, the trail forks; take the left fork to continue on the east side of Arabia Lake. The right fork offers access to the west shore of the lake.

Continuing on the trail, the lake is now on the right. You may see resident wood ducks, great blue herons, or any of the local or migrant waterbirds. The path crosses a couple of exposed rock faces along the way, one of which stretches right to the edge of the water. This is a small, clear lake impounded more than a hundred years ago to support quarry operations. There are some old metal structures standing in the water that date from World War II. Georgia Tech used these, under contract with the US Navy, to test underwater explosives.

Continue south along the lakeshore to the junction with the Mile Rock Trail at the dam.

Turn right at this intersection to continue on the Forest Trail. The path drops down past the stone spillway of the lake to follow Stephenson Creek downstream. The trail runs through a pleasant, moist habitat with many flowering plants, ferns, and lichens. After crossing a couple of footbridges, the trail ends at the junction with a long boardwalk portion of the Arabia Mountain Trail.

Reverse course, walk back to the intersection with the Mile Rock Trail, and turn right. This trail begins by passing through a gazebo beside the first rock cairn. The path is across open granite and is not blazed; rather it has roughly thirty stone cairns that serve as trail markers, without which it would be quite difficult to follow the designated path.

The Mile Rock Trail crosses the Lithonia gneiss in the old rock quarry, where the path is marked with cairns.

The pathway leads across smooth quarried sections, as well as uneven areas over scattered large stones of cut granite. Patches of the red diamorpha are abundant, along with small round pockets that hold water.

At the point the trail turns sharply north, the remains of the old quarry office and weigh station are on the right, with the Arabia Mountain Trail running on the other side of the structure. To stay on the Mile Rock Trail, continue to follow the cairns. Shortly, on the left you have a larger, deeper pool with permanent water. This is the Frog Pond. An information plaque explains the significance of this small water hole.

Upon passing the remains of another historic quarry building, the trail quickly exits the granite to enter a pine and hardwood forested area. The trail is a well-defined path that takes you along an old railroad bed associated with the quarry. Stay to the left where a spur trail turns off to the right. When the trail dead-ends into the paved Arabia Mountain Trail, turn right and walk to the nature center.

Miles and Directions

0.0 Start at the Davidson–Arabia Mountain Nature Center, crossing the short boardwalk.

0.2 Cross the paved Arabia Mountain Trail.

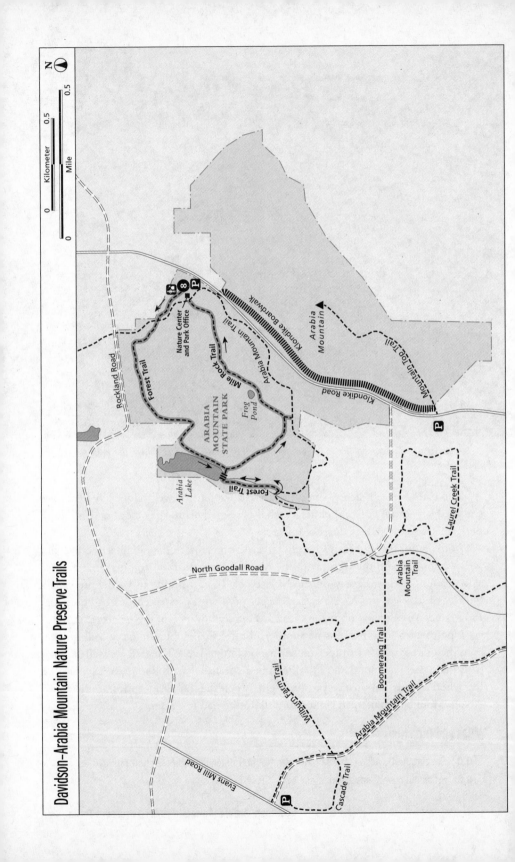

Davidson–Arabia Mountain Nature Preserve Trails

0.7 Cross the small stream that floods the path, and pass the trail junction for the spur leading to the west side of Arabia Lake.

0.8 Arrive at Arabia Lake, cross the exposed rock face, and pass the metal structure standing in the water.

0.9 At the intersection with the Rock Mile Trail, turn right past the lake spillway.

1.2 Reach the turnaround point at the Arabia Mountain Trail junction and reverse course.

1.4 Turn right at the intersection with the Mile Rock Trail and pass through the gazebo.

1.7 Pass the old quarry office and weigh station.

1.8 Skirt the edge of the Frog Pond.

2.1 The historic quarry building is on the right. Leave the open granite for the forested area.

2.2 Pass the intersection with the spur trail to the right.

2.4 Arrive back at the nature center and trailhead.

Options

The **Mountain Top Trail** is a 1.0-mile out-and-back pathway leading from the south parking area to the top of Arabia Mountain. This path also is marked with rock cairns rather than blazes. Once at the top, a 360-degree view is offered of the surrounding lower Piedmont forests.

The **Klondike Boardwalk** spans 0.5 mile from the visitor center parking lot to the south parking lot, paralleling Klondike Road for the entire distance.

The orange-blazed **Cascade Trail** begins at the Evans Mill parking area on the west side of the preserve. It offers a 0.8-mile one-way walk along the shoals of Pole Bridge Creek, across from the historic mill site. Both ends of the trail are anchored to the paved Evans Mill Spur off the Arabia Mountain Trail.

Beginning on the north side of the Evans Mill Spur, across from the end of the Cascade Trail, the **Wilburn Farm Trail** provides a 1.6-mile one-way (with a short loop in the middle) walk through of the remains of the farm that occupied the land beginning in the late 1800s. The other end of this orange-blazed path is at a junction with the Boomerang Trail.

The red-blazed **Boomerang Trail** is a 0.5-mile connector between the multiuse Evans Mill Spur and the main Arabia Mountain Trail.

The **Laurel Creek Trail** is marked with white blazes. This 1.8-mile loop runs off the Arabia Mountain Trail to explore the valley of its namesake creek and the ridge above it.

The **Arabia Mountain Trail** is a 10-foot-wide, 18.4-mile multiuse biking and hiking path. It stretches from the town of Lithonia to Stonecrest Mall, Davidson–Arabia Mountain Nature Preserve, Panola Mountain State Park, and South Rockdale Community Park.

Local Information

Local Events/Attractions

Arabia Mountain National Heritage Area; www.arabiaalliance.org

CHATTAHOOCHEE RIVER NATIONAL RECREATION AREA

The Chattahoochee River begins as a spring in Chattahoochee Gap at the Appalachian Trail, high in the North Georgia mountains near the end of Jacks Knob Trail. It collects water from hundreds of tributaries along its meandering course before it reaches Atlanta as the largest and most important water source for that metropolitan area.

The Chattahoochee River National Recreation Area was established in 1978 to preserve the river corridor and provide recreation under management of the National Park Service. Sixteen tracts of land have been developed for recreation on the 48 miles of river flowing through the north and west regions of metro Atlanta. Four of the tracts with hiking trails are discussed here. Most of the other units have similar hiking trails.

A detailed map of the Chattahoochee River from Buford Dam down to Atlanta is available from the National Park Service. It shows access roads to all the units of land administered by the Park Service. The map can be found at www.nps.gov/chat.

The flow of the Chattahoochee River is controlled for hydroelectric-power generation at Buford Dam. Depending on water releases, the river may be very full or quite low with many rocks exposed in the shoals. The water discharged from Buford Dam is cold—50 to 60 degrees—year-round. The Georgia Department of Natural Resources, Wildlife Resources Division manages the river for a very popular rainbow and brown trout fishery. Visit www.georgiawildlife.com/fishing/ for more information on the fishing.

For more information:

River Through Atlanta Guide Service, 710 Riverside Rd., Roswell 30075; (770) 650-8630; www.riverthroughatlanta.com.

Upper Chattahoochee Riverkeeper, 3 Puritan Mill, 916 Joseph E. Lowery Blvd. NW, Atlanta 30318; (404) 352-9828; www.chattahoochee.org. An independent environmental organization whose mission is to advocate and secure protection of the Chattahoochee River, its tributaries, and its watershed.

The Chattahoochee Cold Water Tailrace Fishery Foundation, Inc., 710 Riverside Rd., Roswell 30075; (770) 650-8630; www.chattahoocheefoodwebs.org. Dedicated to protecting the cold-water trout fishery in the Chattahoochee River and supporting the work of the Georgia Wildlife Resources Division and the National Park Service effort to manage these waters.

9 Red Top Mountain State Park Trails

Red Top Mountain State Park covers 1,776 acres of land on the shores of Allatoona Lake, just a short distance northwest of Atlanta. The US Army Corps of Engineers reservoir has almost 12,000 acres of water and is a popular destination for boaters and anglers from the metro Atlanta region.

The park features boat ramps, a swimming beach, picnic areas, and historic pioneer and mining areas. Abundant deer, squirrels, wild turkeys, and other wildlife are present, along with birding opportunities. The Piedmont forest of oak, hickory, and pine, combined with many wildflowers, make this a fascinating day-hike area.

A total of 16.5 miles of hiking and multiuse trails wind through the park, offering short walks in the forest or longer day treks. The featured hike is on the Homestead Trail.

Start: At the porch of the park office
Distance: 5.6-mile lollipop
Hiking time: About 2.5 hours
Difficulty: Easy to moderate
Trail surface: Dirt; some paved road sections
Best Season: Mar–Dec
Other trail users: Hikers only
Canine compatibility: Leashed dogs permitted
Land status: Georgia DNR, State Parks & Historic Sites Division

Nearest town: Cartersville
Fees and permits: Daily parking fee
Schedule: Park hours, 7 a.m.–10 p.m., year-round
Maps: USGS Allatoona Dam; page-size map of the trails available at the park office
Trail contacts: Red Top Mountain State Park, 50 Lodge Rd. SE, Cartersville 30120; (770) 975-0055; www.gastateparks.org

Finding the trailhead: From Atlanta go north on I-75 to exit 285. Go east on Red Top Mountain Road 1.5 miles; the Homestead Trail starts at the park office. Trailhead GPS: N34 08.883'/W84 42.440'

The Hike

The trailhead for the Homestead Trail is at the park office building. This yellow-blazed trail is the most varied and interesting of all the trails in the park. It leads you through a wide variety of habitats. Mile-marker posts have been placed along the path, a handy reference for the beginning hiker.

The trail begins by alternately descending into hollows with wet-weather streams and climbing onto and over ridgelines. The bottoms have loblolly pines and tulip poplar trees with frequent Christmas ferns in the understory. Scattered throughout the trail are dogwoods and muscadine vines. On the ridges the tree canopy turns to an oak and hickory mix.

Before reaching the 1.1-mile mark, the trail twice shares the path with stretches of the red-blazed Sweet Gum Trail, passes over a boardwalk, and crosses the paved lodge entrance road. Just across the road the Sweet Gum Trail splits off a final time.

The Homestead Trail loops around several coves on Allatoona Lake.

Roughly 100 yards beyond the pavement, the loop starts and goes around to the right (counterclockwise). The path drops down to one of the arms of Allatoona Lake, which comes into view at 0.4 mile beyond the loop junction. From there you climb to a higher ridge providing scenic views of the lake.

Now skirting the lake, you reach a trailside bench that offers an overlook of the reservoir, and then you come to a trail junction. An obvious path leads downhill to the right, but the blue blazes on it are poorly marked. This trail extends down to a point overlooking the lake. From this spot you have a panoramic view of the reservoir and can see Allatoona Dam to the west. The out-and-back walk on the side trail adds 0.4 mile to the hike, while dropping and regaining 70 feet of elevation along the way.

Returning to the yellow-blazed trail, you pass near one of the old homesites that were occupied when iron ore and clay were mined from Red Top Mountain.

You can expect to see deer along any portion of the trail; the wild turkeys are much more wary and difficult to spot. You're sure to see squirrels and many species of birds.

The path loops back around the crest of Red Top Mountain before completing the loop, crossing the paved road, and returning to the park office.

Be aware that the path from the road back to the next junction where the Sweet Gum Trail joins from the left is only blazed in red, despite also carrying the Homestead Trail.

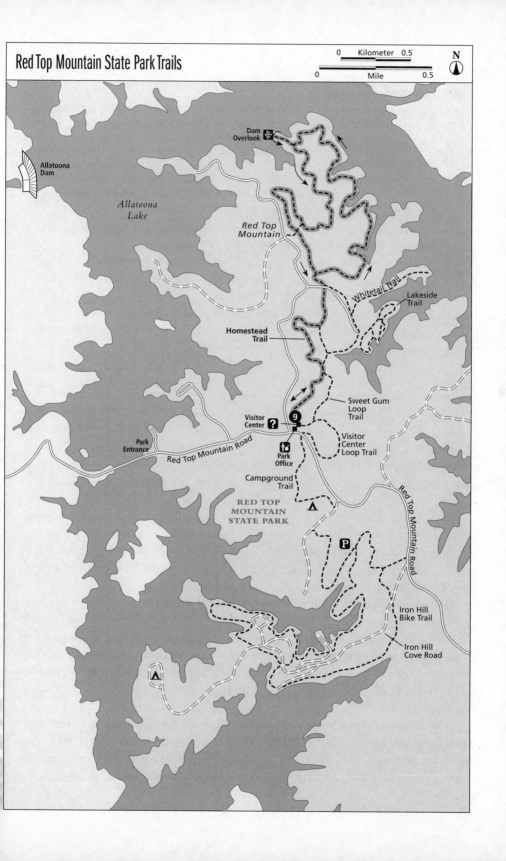

Red Top Mountain State Park Trails

0   Kilometer   0.5

0   Mile   0.5

N

Dam Overlook

Allatoona Dam

Allatoona Lake

Red Top Mountain

Whitetail Trail

Lakeside Trail

Homestead Trail

Sweet Gum Loop Trail

Visitor Center

9

Visitor Center Loop Trail

Park Entrance

Red Top Mountain Road

Park Office

Campground Trail

RED TOP MOUNTAIN STATE PARK

Red Top Mountain Road

P

Iron Hill Bike Trail

Iron Hill Cove Road

Miles and Directions

0.0 Start at the visitor center.

0.4 Join the red-blazed Sweet Gum Trail until it angles off to the right in about 90 yards. Where they join, a patch of mayapple hugs the ground on the right side of the trail.

0.9 Rejoin the Sweet Gum Trail.

1.0 Pass over a boardwalk.

1.1 Cross the paved road that leads to the lodge. The Sweet Gum Trail turns off to the right; continue straight ahead on the yellow-blazed Homestead Trail for 125 yards to where the trail divides; take the right fork to follow the loop counterclockwise.

1.4 Get your first view of Allatoona Lake, with more to follow in the next 1.5 miles. Good views of the lake are especially available in winter and early spring.

1.8 An overlook with a bench provides a very good view of a cove on the reservoir.

2.7 A short trail takes off to the right. (**Option:** Take this 0.4-mile trail out and back for a good view of the lake and Allatoona Dam.)

3.9 The trail makes a U-turn after circling the crest of Red Top Mountain.

4.5 Close the loop and head back to the visitor center.

5.6 Arrive back at the visitor center.

Options

The **Lakeside Trail** is 0.6 mile long, completely barrier free and wheelchair accessible. It is a good trail for anyone interested in wildlife. Bird feeders and bird and mammal nest boxes are placed at appropriate places along the trail. White-tailed deer come right to the trail. They are well conditioned to people and easily seen if you remain quiet. Many birds, including hummingbirds and a variety of songbirds, are attracted to the area. Lake Allatoona is visible throughout most of the walk.

The Vaughn Cabin, a pioneer structure dating from 1869, is on this trail, along with exhibits of vintage farm equipment. The path also passes a boat dock.

Two cross paths make it possible to return to the trailhead without making the entire loop or backtracking. A small field, mixed hardwood–pine forest, and lake edge give the walk an interesting mixture of habitat types.

The green-blazed **Visitor Center Loop Trail** begins at the north end of the park office parking lot on the same path as the Sweet Gum Trail (red blazes). At 165 yards the Sweet Gum Trail forks to the left. The undulating Visitor Center Trail, a 0.6-mile loop, takes you through stands of almost pure loblolly pine and into a forest of large hardwood trees and beside a small stream. There are two observation platforms along the path. The trail ends beside the tennis courts at the south end of the visitor center parking lot.

The **Whitetail Trail** bears white blazes and originates at the visitor center area. This path leads down a ridge and then follows a short hollow toward the lake. From that it climbs to the top of a point running out into Allatoona Lake. The 0.5-mile trail ends at the rocky tip of the point, where you have a view of the lake.

A short side trail leads to a panoramic view of the lake, including a view of Allatoona Dam.

The **Sweet Gum Loop Trail,** marked with red blazes, travels along a dry ridge of white, chestnut, and red oaks, with dogwoods, huckleberries, and other shrubs growing underneath. This is a good place to look for spring wildflowers. The trail overlooks a small, quiet valley. Two observation decks allow you to sit and watch for wildlife.

The very interesting gold-blazed 0.5-mile **Campground Trail** leads from the campground to the park office. It passes an opening in the woods where deer are likely to be seen, crosses three bridges, and passes the stone ruins of an old homestead. The trailhead is located in the campground near comfort station No. 2.

The **Iron Hill Bike Trail** is a multiuse biking and hiking gravel path. This trail makes a 3.9-mile loop through an area that hosted an iron mining community in the nineteenth century. The path follows the shoreline of the lake, passing amid a profusion of native wildlife and plants.

The parking lot for this trail is located off Red Top Mountain Road, on the right 0.5 mile past the campground as you travel to the southeast.

Local Information

Accommodations

Red Top Mountain State Park has a 92-site RV and tent campground, a yurt, and 18 rental cottages.

Organizations

Friends of Red Top Mountain State Park; friendsofredtop.org

10 Amicalola Falls State Park, Appalachian Approach Trail

Amicalola, a Cherokee word meaning "tumbling waters," perfectly describes Amicalola Falls. Formed by Little Amicalola Creek plunging 729 feet in several cascades, it is the highest waterfall east of the Mississippi River and serves as the centerpiece of an 829-acre park.

The state park has seven short hiking trails totaling 4.5 miles and serves as the trailhead for two much longer hikes that leave the property and cross onto Chattahoochee National Forest lands.

The featured hike is a long trek on the Appalachian Approach Trail.

Start: At the Amicalola Falls Visitor Center
Distance: 8.3 miles one way from visitor center to Appalachian Trail at Springer Mountain
Hiking time: About 5 hours
Difficulty: Easy to strenuous
Trail surface: Compacted dirt and rocks
Best season: Mar–Dec
Other trail users: Hikers only in the park; hunters in season on national forest land
Canine compatibility: Dogs permitted in national forest; leashed dogs permitted in the state park
Land status: Georgia DNR, State Parks & Historic Sites Division; Chattahoochee National Forest

Nearest towns: Dahlonega, Ellijay
Fees and permits: Daily parking fee
Maps: USGS Amicalola and Nimblewill; detailed trail map available at visitor center; USDA Forest Service map of Chattahoochee National Forest and Georgia section of Appalachian Trail
Trail contacts: Amicalola Falls State Park and Lodge, 240 Amicalola Falls Park Rd., Dawsonville 30534; (706) 265-4703; www.gastate parks.org; www.georgia-atclub.org

Finding the trailhead: Amicalola Falls State Park Visitor Center is 20 miles east of Ellijay and 14 miles west of Dahlonega on SR 52. Trailhead for the Appalachian Approach Trail is behind the visitor center. Trailhead GPS: N34 33.465'/W84 14.957'

The Hike

The Appalachian Approach Trail begins as you walk through the attractive stone archway behind the visitor center. The blue-blazed trail climbs about 1,000 feet to the parking area above the falls. However, it starts with a gentle grade through a picnic area and along a boardwalk before crossing the road and passing through more picnic sites along Little Amicalola Creek. Upon reaching the Reflection Pool, the trail becomes a paved path.

Where the pavement ends, the trail beings the steep climb up 177 wooden steps to the observation bridge across the creek. At the end of the bridge the trail turns to the

Enjoying the view from the observation bridge on the Foot of the Falls Trail

right to climb another 425 steps to the top of the falls. Here the trail follows a paved path back across the creek to the parking lot for the Len Foote Hike Inn.

Exiting the parking area, the trail now shares the path with the Hike Inn Trail and has both blue and green blazes. Shortly after crossing a road, the Hike Inn Trail splits off to the right, and the Approach Trail reverts to blue blazes only.

In the next 0.5 mile the trail crosses a footbridge, then another road, and exits the state park into the Chattahoochee National Forest. The trail climbs continuously until reaching a clearing on top of Frosty Mountain. Here the path leads between the concrete footings that are all that is left of the old fire tower that once stood on the peak.

Another 0.8 mile brings you to the junction with Len Foote Hike Inn Trail that approaches from the right. From here the trail begins to descend down to Old Bucktown Road in Nimblewill Gap. Next the trail climbs steeply for 1.5 miles to the junction with a side trail to the right leading to a trail shelter.

Continuing to climb, the path makes the final approach up the shoulder of Springer Mountain to an overlook at the point where the Appalachian National Scenic Trail begins at the crest. The spot is marked with a couple of plaques. Beneath one of these a compartment has been built into the side of the rock, and a notebook and pen are stored there. Be sure to sign your name and leave a note for other hikers reaching the point.

This is the turnaround point for heading back to the park. Or, if you have arranged a shuttle, you can continue on the Appalachian Trail for another mile to the parking lot on FS 42 (Alternate Trailhead GPS: N34 38.261' / W84 11.710'). That makes for a 9.2-mile hike. If you choose to head back to the park from Spring Mountain, the trek out and back covers 16.6 miles.

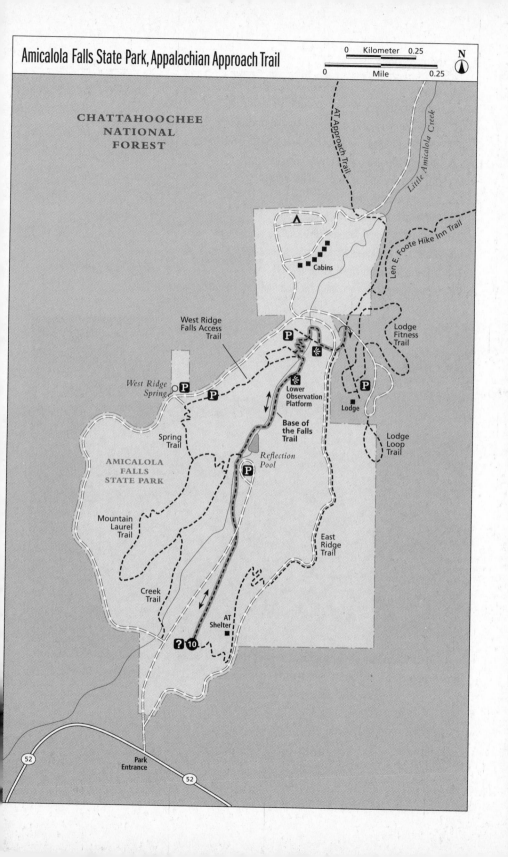

Amicalola Falls State Park, Appalachian Approach Trail

0   Kilometer   0.25

0   Mile   0.25

N

CHATTAHOOCHEE
NATIONAL
FOREST

AT Approach Trail

Little Amicalola Creek

Cabins

Len E. Foote Hike Inn Trail

West Ridge
Falls Access
Trail

Lodge
Fitness
Trail

West Ridge
Spring

Lower
Observation
Platform

Lodge

Base of
the Falls
Trail

Spring
Trail

Reflection
Pool

Lodge
Loop
Trail

AMICALOLA
FALLS
STATE PARK

Mountain
Laurel
Trail

East
Ridge
Trail

Creek
Trail

AT
Shelter

? 10

52

Park
Entrance

52

Miles and Directions

0.0 Start at the visitor center archway.

0.5 Pass the Reflection Pool.

0.7 Begin climbing the 602 steps to the top of the falls.

0.9 Cross the bridge over Little Amicalola Creek at the top of the falls.

1.0 Reach the parking area above the falls.

1.2 The Hike Inn Trail separates to the right.

1.5 Leave the state park.

4.4 Arrive at the crest of Frosty Mountain.

5.0 Pass the junction with the Hike Inn Trail on the right.

5.6 Cross Old Bucktown Road in Nimblewill Gap.

7.0 Pass to the left of the trail shelter.

8.3 Arrive at Springer Mountain, the southern end of the Appalachian Trail.

The panorama from the top of Springer Mountain at the beginning of the Appalachian Trail

11 Amicalola Falls State Park, Len Foote Hike Inn Trail

The Len Foote Hike Inn is located outside of Amicalola State Park on adjacent Chattahoochee National Forest property. However, the facility is managed and maintained by the Georgia State Parks and Historic Sites Division. Visitors can only reach the inn using the hiking trail that originates in the park.

The Len Foote Hike Inn Trail offers a leisurely morning or afternoon trek up to the inn. Once there visitors find soft beds, warm showers, and hot meals awaiting. A library and board games are provided, or one can simply lounge in a chair on the decks enjoying the mountain vista.

This featured hike is a long trek on the Len Foote Hike Inn Trail.

See map page 64.
Start: At the top of the falls in the Hike Inn parking lot
Distance: 5.9 miles one way to the upper junction with the Appalachian Approach Trail
Hiking time: About 3–3.5 hours
Difficulty: Easy to strenuous
Trail surface: Compacted dirt and rocks
Best season: Mar–Dec
Other trail users: Hikers only in the park; hunters in season on national forest land
Canine compatibility: Dogs permitted in national forest; leashed dogs permitted in the state park

Land status: Georgia DNR, State Parks & Historic Sites Division; Chattahoochee National Forest
Nearest towns: Dahlonega, Ellijay
Fees and permits: Daily parking fee
Maps: USGS Amicalola and Nimblewill; detailed trail map available at visitor center; USDA Forest Service map of Chattahoochee National Forest and Georgia section of Appalachian Trail
Trail contacts: Hike Inn; (800) 581-8032; www.Hike-Inn.com

Finding the trailhead: Amicalola Falls State Park is 20 miles east of Ellijay and 14 miles west of Dahlonega on SR 52. The Len Foote Hike Inn Trail begins at the Hike Inn parking area at the top of the waterfall. Trailhead GPS: N34 34.035'/N84 14.610'

The Hike

Lime-green rectangular blazes mark the way for this trail to the Len Foote Hike Inn. The inn, a welcome sight after your hike, offers the opportunity to spend a night in the wilderness without the need for sleeping bag, tent, or other camping gear. If you're staying overnight at the inn, you must check in at the Amicalola State Park Visitor Center and receive your permit by 2 p.m. the day of your reservation to ensure that you complete the hike and return to the inn before dark.

The Hike Inn is named for Leonard E. Foote (1918–89), a consummate conservationist who spent his life in research and management of wildlife. For three decades he was the southeastern field representative of the Wildlife Management Institute.

Guests can only reach the Leonard Foote Hill Inn by walking.

In the evening, guests at the inn are treated to entertaining programs dealing with the natural history of the area, including illustrated discussions of birds and flowers. Visitors can also learn about the conservation techniques used to manage the facility efficiently.

From the parking area above the falls, follow along with the Appalachian Approach Trail across the paved road where the path at the stone wall directs you into the woods.

Where the Approach Trail splits off to the left, follow the green blazes to the right. It is a steady climb to the ridge crest on a well-maintained and easy-to-follow trail. You will cross four ridges, but none of them are very steep.

The forest floor has been relatively clear to this point, but now you encounter a thick growth of low vegetation in summer consisting of grasses, herbaceous plants, and many young sassafras trees. At the crest of this first ridge a couple of log benches provide a breather and a good vista in the winter, when leaves are off the trees.

Changes in vegetation will continue throughout the hike as you go from west- to east-facing and south- to north-facing ridge exposures. In spring look for the abundance of blooming wildflowers, including trailing arbutus, sessile and Vasey's trilliums, jack-in-the-pulpits, and pink lady's slippers. Among the trees and shrubs are silver bells, dogwoods, redbuds, buckeyes, yellow poplars, and mountain laurel. Along the trail are glades of New York ferns as well as marginal wood, lady, Christmas, and bracken ferns, along with some spleenworts.

You might be surprised at the number of seedling and sprouting American chestnuts along the trail. Unfortunately they will soon succumb to the chestnut blight that has been killing the trees since the 1930s.

Mammals in the area include black bears, white-tailed deer, foxes, squirrels, chipmunks, raccoons, and opossums along with smaller deer mice, shrews, and moles. Most are only seen as tracks in the soft ground or as signs of feeding.

This is an excellent birding trail in spring and fall for migrating warblers, grosbeaks, orioles, and others. Besides the migrant birds there are many resident species like warblers, towhees, wrens, hawks, owls and, at higher elevations, ravens.

On the crest of each ridge you get good fall and winter vistas to the southeast down the valley of Cochrans Creek. Just before you begin the final ascent to the lodge, the trail passes through a wet area with five boardwalks, finishing off by crossing another stream, Cochrans Falls Creek, on a footbridge.

At 4.9 miles you reach the front door of the Hike Inn.

If you are day hiking, be sure to walk the trail around the right side of the lodge to the fabulous overlook behind the building. You can then retrace your path back to the parking lot for a day hike of 9.9 miles. Another option is to continue another 1.0 mile past the inn up to the trail junction with the Appalachian Approach Trail. Turning left at that point creates a loop walk of 10.9 miles back to the parking lot.

Miles and Directions

0.0 Start at the designated parking area at top of the falls. The green-blazed Hike Inn and blue-blazed Appalachian Approach Trails share the path.

0.3 The Appalachian Approach Trail angles off to the left.

0.6 Exit the state park into the Chattahoochee National Forest.

0.9 Reach a bench rest, winter vista, and a section of trail with many sassafras trees.

2.6 Cross a footbridge over Cochrans Creek.

3.2 Arrive at a second bench rest with a winter view of the mountains to the south.

3.9 Pass through a rock outcrop with a vista to the south.

4.5 Cross five boardwalks over the creek bottom in the next 110 yards, then a bridge over Cochrans Falls Creek.

4.8 Reach the junction with the Fire Break Trail on the right.

4.9 Arrive at the Len Foote Hike Inn.

5.0 Pass the other end of the Fire Break Trail.

5.9 Arrive at the junction with Appalachian Approach Trail.

Options

The **Creek Trail** follows the course of Little Amicalola Creek on the west, upstream to the reflection pool at the base of the waterfalls. The 0.6-mile trail has yellow blazes. It stays up on the ridge side for most of the way and is rated moderate to difficult.

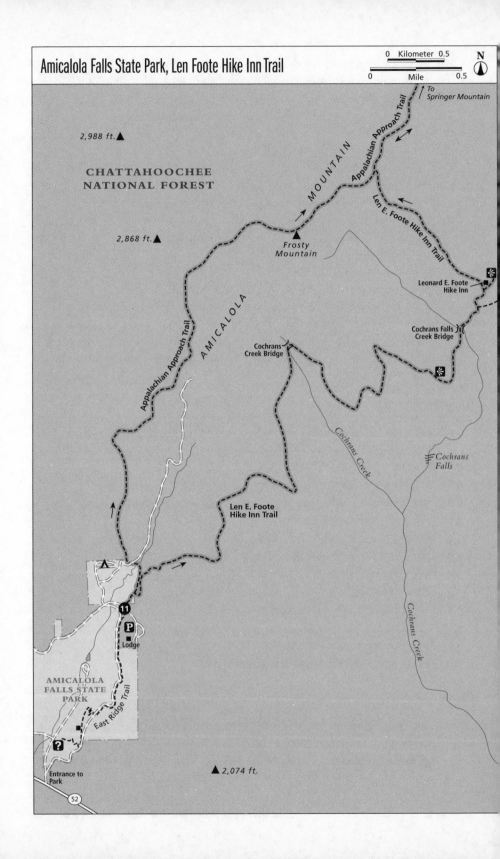

Amicalola Falls State Park, Len Foote Hike Inn Trail

0 Kilometer 0.5

0 Mile 0.5

N

To
Springer Mountain

2,988 ft. ▲

MOUNTAIN

Appalachian Approach Trail

CHATTAHOOCHEE
NATIONAL FOREST

Len E. Foote Hike Inn Trail

2,868 ft. ▲

Frosty
Mountain ▲

Leonard E. Foote
Hike Inn

AMICALOLA

Cochrans Falls
Creek Bridge

Appalachian Approach Trail

Cochrans
Creek Bridge

Cochrans Creek

Cochrans
Falls

Len E. Foote
Hike Inn Trail

A

11

P
■ Lodge

Cochrans Creek

AMICALOLA
FALLS STATE
PARK

East Ridge Trail

■

? ▲ 2,074 ft.

Entrance to
Park

52

The **Spring Trail** is a 0.4-mile path marked with orange blazes. Rated moderate, the path connects the West Ridge Falls Access Trail parking area to the Mountain Laurel Loop Trail.

The green-blazed **Mountain Laurel Loop Trail** is a 1.0-mile, moderate to difficult trail. The path runs along the top of the ridge to the west of Little Amicalola Creek. Access is from the Creek or Spring Trail.

The **West Ridge Falls Access Trail** is an easy 0.2-mile path running from the parking area on the drive to the top of the falls to the observation bridge over the creek halfway up the falls. The trail surface is made of recycled rubber tires and is wheelchair accessible.

The unblazed **East Ridge Trail** offers a 1.0-mile hike to the top of the falls on the eastern side. It begins at the visitor center, climbs through woodlands, and then follows a service road to the Hike Inn parking area. This was the original path of the Appalachian Approach Trail to the top of the falls.

The **Lodge Loop Trail** covers 0.25 mile of easy asphalt pathway to the south of the lodge's entrance. The loop is lighted and wheelchair accessible.

The **Lodge Fitness Trail** spans a 1.0-mile loop to the north of the lodge. There are twenty exercise stations spaced along the path.

Local Information

Accommodations

The Amicalola Falls Lodge offers 56 motel-style rooms, and its Maple Restaurant serves three meals daily. The state park also offers 14 fully equipped cottages and a 24-site campground; www.gastateparks.org/info/amicalola/.

The Len Foote Hike Inn has 20 guest rooms available by reservation only. Breakfast and dinner are served in the inn dining hall; www.hike-inn.com.

12 Appalachian Trail in Georgia

The Appalachian Trail (AT) is one of the longest continually marked trails in the world. Beginning at Springer Mountain in Georgia, the path ends at Mount Katahdin in Maine. Congress authorized the Appalachian Trail as the first National Scenic Trail in 1968. The Appalachian Trail Conference now has responsibility for the trail.

A long-trail concept along the Appalachian Mountains grew out of a 1921 proposal by forester and land-use planner Benton MacKaye. For 16 years, Civilian Conservation Corps (CCC) members, hiking clubs, and other volunteers worked to see MacKaye's dream come true.

On August 14, 1937, the final 2 miles were opened in Maine, completing the 2,054-mile trail from Georgia to Maine. The original terminus in Georgia was Mount Oglethorpe, 20 miles farther south than today's Springer Mountain.

The trail has undergone many changes in the ensuing years. Storms, changes in land use, and other factors have made it necessary to reroute sections of the trail. This is an ongoing process.

Because of the multiple-approach paths on public land, this trail presents a many-faceted hiking opportunity for thousands of hikers each year. It is estimated that about 10 percent of them take 4 to 6 months to actually hike all the way to Maine. The rest discontinue the hike at varying distances up the Blue Ridge. Others hike only portions of the trail, and some hike only a few miles to some interesting point, usually using any one of the approach trails.

The beauty of the Appalachian Trail is that it seems to accommodate all. This concept is best described by the plaque on Springer Mountain that reads GEORGIA TO MAINE—A FOOTPATH FOR THOSE WHO SEEK FELLOWSHIP WITH THE WILDERNESS.

Start: From the visitor center in Amicalola State Park, take the 8.3-mile approach trail to Springer Mountain, the AT's official southern terminus.
Distance: 75.4 miles one way
Hiking time: About 4-5 days
Difficulty: Moderate to strenuous
Trail surface: Dirt and forest loam, with some rock portions
Best season: Mar-June; Oct-Dec
Other trail users: Hunters in season
Canine compatibility: Dogs permitted in national forest portions; leashed dogs permitted in wildlife management area portions
Land status: Primarily Chattahoochee National Forest

Nearest towns: Five paved highway crossings lead to Dahlonega, Cleveland, Blairsville, Helen, and Clayton.
Fees and permits: Daily parking fee at Amicalola State Park; arrangements can be made for longer term parking at the visitor center.
Schedule: The Georgia section of the trail can be hiked year-round.
Maps: USGS Amicalola, Nimblewill, Noontootla, Suches, Neels Gap, Cowrock, Jacks Gap, Tray Mountain, Macedonia, and Hightower Bald; *The Appalachian Trail in Georgia* (map and brochure), Georgia Appalachian Trail Club, Inc.; *The Guide to the Appalachian Trail in North Carolina and Georgia,* the Appalachian Trail Conservancy; Appalachian

Trail–Chattahoochee National Forest Georgia, USDA Forest Service

Trail contacts: Georgia Appalachian Trail Club Inc., PO Box 654, Atlanta 30301; (404) 494-0968; www.georgia-atclub.org

USDA Forest Service, Forest Supervisor, 1755 Cleveland Hwy., Gainesville 30501; (770) 297-3000; www.fs.usda.gov/conf

Georgia Department of Natural Resources (DNR); www.gadnr.org

Georgia State Parks and Historic Sites Division; www.gastateparks.org

Georgia Wildlife Resources Division, Game Management Section, 2150 Dawsonville Hwy., Gainesville 30501; (770) 535-5700;

www.gohuntgeorgia.com (for hunting season information)

Special considerations: Anyone planning to hike long sections of the trail should first contact the Georgia Appalachian Trail Club for current information.

Because the route of the Appalachian Trail in Georgia is excellent black bear habitat, it is necessary to take precautions with food at campsites. Hang food from a tree limb at least 10 feet off the ground, and do not leave food in your tent if you are away from it for several hours. There is little physical danger from bears, which are usually only a nuisance at heavily used campsites.

Finding the trailhead: The southern terminus for the trail is remote Springer Mountain, near FS 42. Since this area is difficult to reach by automobile, the recommended start is at the Appalachian Approach Trailhead from the visitor center in Amicalola Falls State Park. To reach the park from Dahlonega, go 14 miles west on SR 52. Trailhead GPS: N34 33.465'/W84 14.957'

The Hike

A wilderness hike in rugged terrain along a clearly marked trail for many miles with appropriately spaced shelters, scenic vistas, wildlife, and a variety of hiking adventures and challenges on a world-famous trail makes the Appalachian one of the most popular of all hiking destinations.

Spring and early summer offers displays of azalea, mountain laurel, rhododendron, and many other wildflowers. October brings spectacular leaf color. Mountain scenery that is hidden from view by summer foliage is open in winter, with many eye-catching vistas.

The Georgia section of the trail runs from Springer Mountain to Bly Gap on the North Carolina state line. There are fourteen primitive shelters spaced about a day's hike apart on the trail. Most are three-sided and are close to water.

The oldest shelter, located atop Blood Mountain, was built by the CCC in the 1930s. This four-sided stone structure has a fireplace and a sleeping platform. Some of the shelters are well off the main trail. Whitly Gap shelter at Wildcat Mountain is 1.1 miles off the AT on a well-marked, blue-blazed trail. Other shelters are as much as 0.3 mile off the AT on side trails.

Trail relocation to prevent overuse causes variations in mileage from year to year.

From the visitor center, at an elevation about 1,800 feet, hike the blue-blazed trail past the waterfall. Continue to climb along old roads for about 3.5 miles to Frosty Mountain. Go through Nimblewill Gap, up to Black Mountain, and through another

Appalachian Trail in Georgia

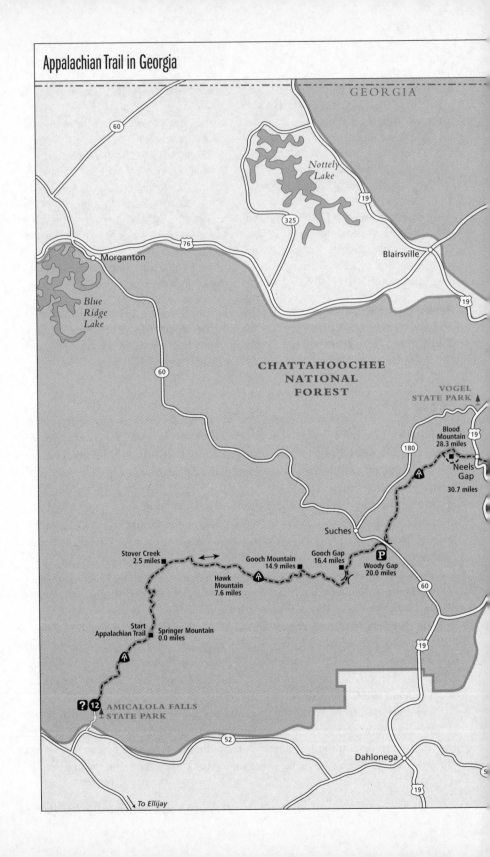

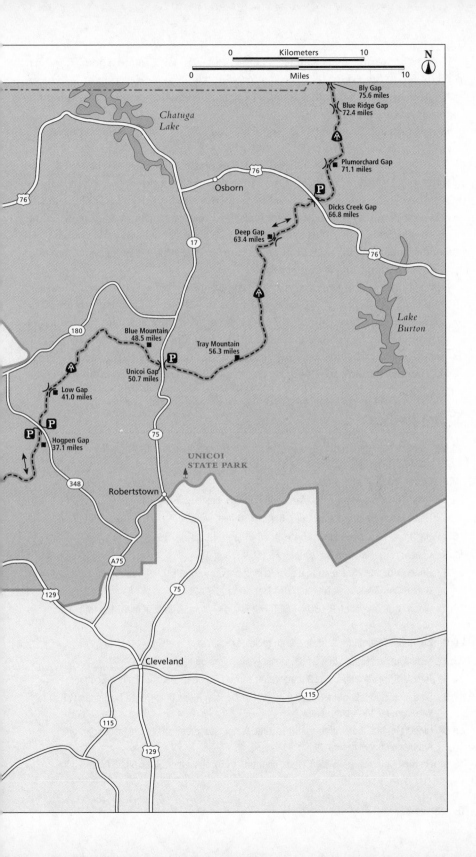

Kilometers 0 10

Miles 0 10

N

Chatuga Lake

Bly Gap
75.6 miles

Blue Ridge Gap
72.4 miles

Plumorchard Gap
71.1 miles

76

Osborn

Dicks Creek Gap
66.8 miles

Deep Gap
63.4 miles

17

76

Lake Burton

180

Blue Mountain
48.5 miles

Tray Mountain
56.3 miles

Unicoi Gap
50.7 miles

Low Gap
41.0 miles

Hogpen Gap
37.1 miles

75

UNICOI
STATE PARK

348

Robertstown

A75

129

75

Cleveland

115

115

129

3,200-foot-high gap where Gilmer, Fannin, and Dawson Counties join. The final uphill stretch to Springer Mountain is a 580-foot climb to an elevation of 3,782 feet. The trail then passes through a forest of the stunted oaks to the rock marking the beginning of the Appalachian Trail.

Jarrard Gap and Slaughter Gap Approach Trails begin at Lake Winfield Scott, 4.5 miles east of Suches on SR 180.

The Byron Herbert Reece Farm and Cultural Center Area is about 0.4 mile north on US 19/129 from Neels Gap. From this trailhead the Freeman Trail climbs 0.7 mile across the shoulder of Blood Mountain to the Appalachian Trail, a moderate 400-foot climb. To the right is a stiff climb to the top of Blood Mountain. To the left the trail drops down 1.0 mile to Neels Gap. This spur trail and parking area were designed to take pressure away from Neels Gap and the Walasi-Yi Center, where hiking and backpacking supplies are available.

Jacks Knob Trail provides access to the Appalachian Trail at Chattahoochee Gap.

Dockery Lake Trail is a 3.4-mile trail from the Dockery Lake Recreation Area. The recreation area is on SR 60, 12 miles north of Dahlonega. The trailhead is at the parking lot for the picnic area. This trail climbs about 400 feet to Millers Gap on the Appalachian Trail. This hike goes up Pigeon Roost Creek, a tributary of Waters Creek. The trail is moderate along the creek and becomes strenuous in the last climb to the gap.

Miles and Directions

0.0 Springer Mountain is the southern terminus of Appalachian Trail. Begin on the white-blazed trail to Bly Gap, NC.

2.5 Stover Creek Shelter; water.

4.1 Three Forks: elevation 2,500 feet; water; FS 58; limited parking.

7.6 Hawk Mountain trail shelter: elevation 3,380 feet; water.

8.1 Hightower Gap: elevation 2,854 feet; FS 69 and 42.

11.6 Cooper Gap: elevation 2,820 feet; FS 80, 42, and 15.

14.9 Gooch Mountain Shelter and a good spring are on a short side trail to the left.

16.3 Gooch Gap Shelter: elevation 2,784 feet; water; FS 42.

19.9 Woody Gap: elevation 3,160 feet; SR 60; first paved road, parking area, and trail information sign.

20.9 Big Cedar Mountain; good view from rock ledges.

22.9 Miller Gap: elevation 2,980 feet; Dockery Lake Trail on right.

25.5 Jarrard Gap: elevation 3,310 feet; water; Jarrard Gap Trail to Lake Winfield Scott.

27.2 Slaughter Gap: elevation 3,850 feet; end of Duncan Ridge Trail; Coosa Backcountry Trail to Vogel State Park; water nearby.

28.1 Blood Mountain: elevation 4,458 feet; no water; stone trail shelter; highest point on Appalachian Trail in Georgia.

29.5 Flatrock Gap: elevation 3,460 feet; spur trail to Byron Herbert Reece Trail; Freeman Trail.

The view from the top of Springer Mountain at the start of the Appalachian Trail

30.5   Neels Gap: elevation 3,125 feet; Walasi-Yi Center with hostel for through-hikers only from March to Memorial Day. The center also has a hiking and camping outfitting store with books, maps, and snacks.

33.9   Wolf Laurel Top; campsite and views.

35.3   Cowrock Mountain: elevation 3,852 feet; vistas from rock outcrops.

36.0   Tesnatee Gap: elevation 3,120 feet; SR 348 (Russell Scenic Highway); Logan Turnpike Trail, parking.

36.7 Wildcat Mountain: elevation 3,730 feet; Whitly Gap trail shelter is about 1 mile south on a blue-blazed trail; water; good views; Raven Cliffs Wilderness.

36.9 Hogpen Gap: elevation 3,480 feet; SR 348; parking, interpretive signs and markers.

41.1 Low Gap: elevation 3,032 feet; trail shelter; water.

46.1 Chattahoochee Gap: elevation 3,520 feet; water; beginning of the Chattahoochee River; Jacks Knob Trail to SR 180 and Brasstown Bald.

48.3 Blue Mountain: elevation 4,020 feet; trail shelter; water.

50.5 Unicoi Gap: elevation 2,949 feet; SR 17/75; parking.

53.3 Indian Grave Gap: elevation 3,120; FS 283; Andrews Cove Trail to Andrews Cove Recreation Area.

54.0 Junction with FS 79: elevation 3,400 feet; road leads down to Robertstown and Helen.

54.9 Tray Gap: elevation 3,841 feet; FR 79.

55.7 Tray Mountain: elevation 4,430 feet; trail shelter; water; rock outcrops and scenic views; only a few feet lower than Blood Mountain; Tray Mountain Wilderness.

61.3 Addis Gap: elevation 3,300 feet; FS 26; campsite; water.

63.1 Deep Gap Shelter and water in a piped spring are on a 0.3-mile trail to the right.

66.5 Dicks Creek Gap: elevation 2,675 feet, US 76; parking; picnic area.

70.9 Plumorchard Gap: elevation 3,100 feet; unique trail shelter put in place by helicopter; water.

72.4 Blue Ridge Gap: elevation 3,020 feet; FS 72.

75.4 Bly Gap: elevation 3,840 feet; North Carolina line; there is no road access to this gap as you leave Georgia.

13 Hard Labor Creek State Park Trails

Hard Labor Creek State Park is a 5,864-acre facility situated to the north of I-20, between Covington and Madison in eastern Georgia. Local lore offers two sources for the park's name. One ascribes the name's origin to antebellum slaves who worked in the summer sun in surrounding plantation fields, while the other attributes it to Native Americans who found the stream hard to cross.

The park is best known for its golf course, fishing lakes, swimming beach, and rental cabins. There also are two interconnecting hiking trails that pass through farmland abandoned in the mid-1930s. Additionally, 22 miles of equestrian trails wind through the park.

The featured trail is a joint trek on the Brantley Nature and Beaverpond Nature Trails.

Start: About 100 yards in front of the office/trading post
Distance: 2.2-mile loop
Hiking time: About 1.5 hours
Difficulty: Easy
Trail surface: Dirt with leaf litter
Best season: Year-round
Other trail users: Hikers only
Canine compatibility: Leashed dogs permitted
Land status: Georgia DNR, State Parks & Historic Sites Division

Nearest town: Rutledge
Fees and permits: Daily parking fee
Schedule: Park hours 7 a.m.–10 p.m., year-round
Maps: USGS Rutledge North; trail maps available at the office/trading post
Trail contacts: Hard Labor Creek State Park, 5 Hard Labor Creek Rd., Rutledge 30663; (706) 557-3001; www.gastateparks.org

Finding the trailhead: From I-20 at exit 105, go north on Newborn Road 2.8 miles to Rutledge and continue 2.5 miles on Fairplay Road to Knox Chapel Road. Turn left and go 0.4 mile to Campground Road. Turn right; the office/trading post is 0.1 mile on the right. The trailhead for Brantley Nature Trail is about 100 yards in front of the office on the left of the road to the campground. Trailhead GPS: N33 39.889'/W83 36.354'

The Hike

The 1.0-mile Brantley Nature and 1.1-mile Beaverpond Nature Trails are most practically walked as a single hike. Both are loop trails that are joined by a 70-yard connector. Also, the Beaverpond Nature Trail does not have a separate trailhead of its own.

The trails meander through a mature, second-growth mainly pine-oak forest. However, bridges across small, eroded ravines and terraces in the woods are reminders that this was farmland until abandoned in the mid-1930s.

Wildlife you may encounter includes deer, turkeys, armadillos, and squirrels. Waterfowl and beavers can be found around the park's ponds and lakes.

A giant poplar tree stands on the left of the path just after the start of the Beaverpond Nature Trail loop.

The Brantley Nature Trail begins by descending a ridge from the trailhead. Along the way it passes through an exposed rock formation and then drops steeply to the bottom along a tributary of Hard Labor Creek.

Hard Labor Creek State Park Trails

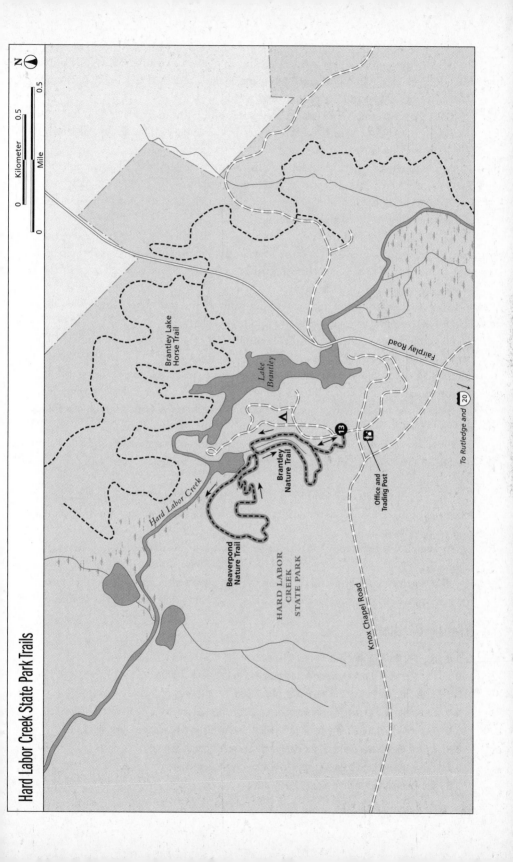

Loblolly pine, several oak species, hickories, dogwood, sourwood, yellow poplar, and beech are all present. Undergrowth plants include redbud, gooseberry, muscadine, Christmas ferns, wood ferns, and pickerel weeds.

The rare piedmont barren strawberry grows along this trail as well. This low plant spreads by subsurface stems like the cultivated strawberry. The five-petaled white flowers bloom from April to June.

At the junction where the loop begins on the Brantley Trail, take the right fork. The trail next crosses a footbridge, just before reaching the connector path to the Beaverpond Trail. At this intersection turn right, walk 70 yards, and turn right again at the beginning of the Beaverpond loop.

The Beaverpond Nature Trail is much like the Brantley Nature Trail, except that it includes areas of older trees and the beaver pond. Roughly 50 yards past the beginning of the loop, a very large yellow poplar is on the left, about 20 yards from the trail. The tree is well over 5 feet in diameter.

Next, the beaver pond appears on the right of the trail. The path crosses three bridges over gullies as it runs long the pond.

Standing water in the pond killed a number of trees that have become excellent habitat for cavity-nesting birds, including the colorful wood duck. The pond is almost completely covered with vegetation and is a favorite place for quiet birding. Pileated and other species of woodpeckers, wading birds, and flycatchers often are observed.

Beyond the pond the trail continues to parallel the creek bottom, which is full of pickerel weed.

Once the trail veers up out of the bottom, it crosses two more bridges and then reaches a sharp left turn. A bent tree at this location forms a perfect natural bench for taking a break.

The rest of the Beaverpond loop stays up on the ridge side, crossing three more bridges. Just prior to closing the loop, the path skirts a rock pile that was the foundation of an old building.

At the close of the loop turn right, and back at the Brantley Trail, take another right turn.

This portion of the hike also is up on the ridge side. After crossing another bridge, the path arrives at the close of this loop. Turn right and walk back to the trailhead.

Miles and Directions

0.0 Start at the Brantley Nature Trail trailhead.

0.1 Pass through the rock outcrop and descend to the creek bottom.

0.2 Take the right fork at the beginning of the loop.

0.4 Cross the bridge over the small branch and turn right to reach the Beaverpond Nature Trail.

0.5 Turn right onto the Beaverpond Nature Trail and at 50 yards pass the huge poplar tree.

0.6 Reach the beaver pond on the right and the creek bottom beyond.

0.7 Leave the wetland area and start to climb a well-forested hillside.

0.8 Turn sharply left at the natural bench tree.

Armadillos are just one of the species that may be spied on the Brantley Nature Trail.

1.4 Pass the old building foundation.

1.6 Close the loop on the Beaverpond Nature Trail; follow the connector back to the Brantley Nature Trail and turn right.

1.9 Cross the last footbridge on the trails.

2.0 Close the loop on the Brantley Nature Trail; turn sharply right.

2.2 Arrive back at the trailhead.

Local Information

Food / Lodging

Hard Labor Creek State Park has 20 rental cottages, 46 regular campsites, and 11 horse campsites; (800) 864-7275; www.gastateparks.org.

14   Charlie Elliott Wildlife Center Trails

The 6,400-acre Charlie Elliott Wildlife Center encompasses the Marben Public Fishing Area (PFA), the Clybel Wildlife Management Area (WMA), and the Charlie Elliott Visitor Center and Conference Center. This is a must-visit area for hiking, birding, fishing, and family outings.

Before being purchased by the Georgia Department of Natural Resources, the tract was used as a private hunting and fishing retreat.

Today the wildlife center is a museum of the history of modern conservation in Georgia, demonstrated in the life of conservationist, wildlife administrator, and outdoors writer Charlie Elliott. The WMA and PFA provide public access to hunting and fishing. The property contains twenty man-made lakes that are open to fishing under varying regulations. It is worth noting that one of those, Margery Lake, has produced the No. 2 and No. 5 biggest largemouth bass ever caught in Georgia. Those lunkers respectively weighed 18 pounds, 1 ounce, and 17 pounds, 4 ounces.

Five short trails within the no-hunting safety zone of the wildlife center total 5.4 miles and provide easy walking as they pass through a variety of habitats from dense woodlands, open fields, and lakeshores to granite outcrops with unique fauna and flora. Additionally, there is a 5.7-mile multiuse trail that meanders through the WMA grounds.

The featured hike is the Clubhouse Trail.

Start: At a shared trailhead at the visitor center
Distance: 1.9-mile lollipop
Hiking time: About 1–1.5 hours
Difficulty: Easy
Trail surface: Soil and loam
Best season: Apr–June; Sept–Nov
Other trail users: Hikers only
Canine compatibility: Leashed dogs permitted
Land status: Georgia DNR, Wildlife Resources Division

Nearest towns: Mansfield, Monticello
Fees and permits: No fees or permits to use the hiking trails
Schedule: Trails open year-round; visitor center open 9 a.m.–4:30 p.m. Tues-Sat, except on state holidays
Maps: USGS Farrar; trail map available at the visitor center or online
Trail contacts: Charlie Elliott Wildlife Center, 543 Elliott Trail, Mansfield 30055; (770) 784-3059; www.georgiawildlife.com/node/694

Finding the trailhead: From Mansfield travel 3 miles south, or 14 miles north from Monticello, on SR 11 and turn southwest on Marben Farm Road. At 0.8 mile turn right on Elliott Trail and proceed to the visitor center parking area. The trailhead is at the walkway leading to the visitor center. Trailhead GPS: N33 27.760'/W83 44.028'

The Hike

Starting at the trailhead, the path turns sharply left at the wooden direction sign 50 yards into the hike. This also is the junction where the Granite Outcrop Trail splits

A view of Clubhouse Lake from the western shore

off to the right. The blazes on the trail now are red. From here the path curves back to the left around and behind the visitor center, where it crosses two short bridges while dropping into a creek valley full of granite boulders. At the bottom the trail crosses the creek on a third bridge and reaches the junction with the white-blazed Pigeonhouse Trail on the left.

Next the path climbs quickly up the opposite side of the creek bottom to run for a short distance on the ridge crest. Upon reaching the next trail junction, turn right to walk the loop in a counterclockwise direction. At this point the trail drops sharply downhill, ending the descent on some wooden steps that bring you to the shore of Clubhouse Lake.

The trail now crosses one of the feeder creeks at the head of the lake and begins skirting along the steep hillside between the water and the conference center buildings. Through here the trail has some wild ginger, or heartleaf, along the path and passes close to several very large beech trees.

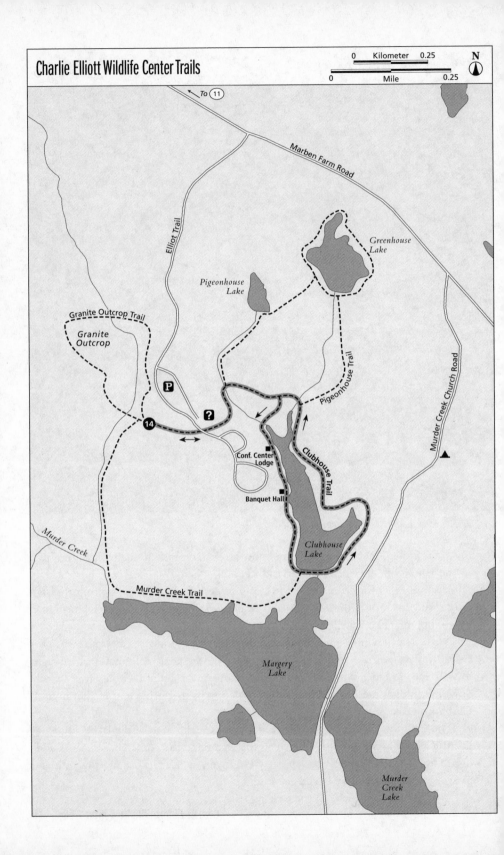

Charlie Elliott Wildlife Center Trails

To (11)

Marben Farm Road

Elliott Trail

Greenhouse Lake

Pigeonhouse Lake

Granite Outcrop Trail

Granite Outcrop

Pigeonhouse Trail

Murder Creek Church Road

P

?

14

Conf. Center Lodge

Clubhouse Trail

Banquet Hall

Murder Creek

Clubhouse Lake

Murder Creek Trail

Margery Lake

Murder Creek Lake

0   Kilometer   0.25

0   Mile   0.25

N

Upon reaching the lake dam, the yellow-blazed Murder Creek Trail approaches from the right. Continue to follow the red blazes across the dam, past the fishing pier, to the opposite side.

Climb the set of stairs beside the Brooke Ager Discovery Building and turn left, following the lakeshore.

Shortly you pass through a large boulder field and then, near the upper end of the lake, an old abandoned deer stand is visible in a tree just off the trail. Soon the white blazes of the other end of the Pigeonhouse Trail are seen on the right at a trail junction.

The path now crosses the other tributary stream entering the lake, before rounding the upper end of the water to close the loop.

Turn right at this junction to return to the trailhead.

Miles and Directions

0.0 Leave the trailhead and turn left at the direction sign.

0.2 Cross the creek and pass the first junction with the Pigeonhouse Trail.

0.3 Reach the loop junction and turn sharply right down the hill.

0.4 Descend a set of wooden steps to the lakeshore, then cross the bridge over the feeder stream entering the lake.

0.5 Pass the conference center buildings on the right.

0.8 Reach the lake's dam and the junction with the Murder Creek Trail.

0.9 Climb the steps beside the Brooke Ager Discovery Building.

1.1 Pass the boulder pile on the right.

1.4 Just before reaching the second junction with the Pigeonhouse Trail, an abandoned deer stand is in a tree overlooking the trail.

1.5 Close the loop and turn right for the trailhead.

1.9 Arrive back at the trailhead.

Options

The **Granite Outcrop Trail** shares the path with the Clubhouse Trail for 50 yards to a wooden orientation sign. This blue-blazed trail then runs to the right. The path forms a 1.1-mile loop that runs over two ridges and circles a large granite formation.

The 5.7-mile **Multiuse Trail** forms a loop through the more open areas of the hunting grounds on Marben Farms WMA. It is open to hiking, horses, and bicycles.

The yellow-blazed **Murder Creek Trail** follows that stream for 0.9 mile to connect the Granite Outcrop and the Clubhouse Trails.

The **Pigeonhouse Trail** loops northward to pass close by Pigeonhouse and Greenhouse Lakes. Both ends of this white-blazed, 1.2-mile trail intersect the Clubhouse Trail.

15 High Falls State Park Trails

High Falls State Park covers 1,050 acres in Monroe County on the shores of High Falls Lake. The impoundment is formed by an old rock dam on the Towaliga River. The river derives its name from the Creek Indian language and translates as "roasted scalps." Those Native Americans were known to scalp their enemies and used the area around High Falls on the river to dry and preserve those trophies.

Waterfalls below the lake drop almost 100 feet in multiple cascades over granite outcrops. These shoals give the area and the state park their names. This is an area of remarkable natural beauty and historic significance, with something of interest throughout the year, including spring wildflowers, fishing, fall colors, and bird migrations.

The rockwork below the river dam is a remnant of the hydropower operation that continued in operation until the mid-twentieth century. Previously there had been a gristmill at the site that was burned during the Civil War and rebuilt in 1866. The park office has excellent historical information on the many businesses that once flourished on the power supplied by the falling water.

The park features picnic and camping areas, boat ramps, playgrounds, miniature golf, a swimming pool, and fishing areas on the lake and river. Three hiking trails varying in length and difficulty provide access to the falls, as well as to historical and natural areas of the park.

The featured hike is a combination trek on the 0.7-mile Historic and 1.9-mile Tranquil Trails.

Start: At a parking area on the left side of Towaliga River Drive on the southwest side of the river
Distance: 2.6-mile double loop
Hiking time: About 1–1.5 hours
Difficulty: Easy to moderate
Trail surface: Loam with leaf litter; occasional rocky areas
Best season: Mar–Dec
Other trail users: Hikers only
Canine compatibility: Leashed dogs permitted

Land status: Georgia DNR, State Parks & Historic Sites Division
Nearest town: Forsyth
Fees and permits: Daily parking fee
Schedule: Park hours, 7 a.m.–10 p.m., year-round
Maps: USGS High Falls; detailed maps of the park and trails available from the park office
Trail contacts: High Falls State Park, 76 High Falls Park Dr., Jackson 30233; (478) 993-3053; www.gastateparks.org

Finding the trailhead: From exit 198 on I-75, go east 1.5 miles on High Falls Road to the park entrance. To reach the trailhead for the Historic and Tranquil Trails, turn right on Towaliga River Drive at the park entrance sign. The parking area is at 0.2 mile on the left. The Historic Trail is on the north side of the road, and the Tranquil Trail runs to the south. Trailhead GPS: N33 10.602'/W84 00.968'

The Hike

The Historic and Tranquil Trails provide samples of all the habitats, history, and scenic views that the park has to offer. The hardwood forests of the yellow-blazed Tranquil Trail are home to deer, turkeys, squirrels, foxes, skunks, and many songbirds. The Historic Trail provides views of the shoals on the river and passes amid the ruins of the old canal and hydroelectric powerhouse that were used in conjunction with the rock dam.

Start the hike at the parking area on the left side of Towaliga River Drive. Begin by walking north across the Canal Dam on the Historic Trail. There are no blazes on this path, but it is easily followed.

As you walk with the canal on the left, the opposite side is covered with a thick stand of bamboo cane. To the right the hillside drops sharply toward the river. After passing the junction where the loop turns down the hillside, continue straight ahead. Next, cross High Falls Road to a millstone at the old mill site. The stub of the old Alabama Bridge extends out over the river, offering a good view upstream toward the rock dam.

Retrace your route back to the loop junction and turn left down the hill. Two observation decks on this portion of the path offer views of Towaliga Falls. A bit farther along, the trail reaches the ruins of the powerhouse on the left. Just beyond, a connector trail descends sharply to the left down to the picnic and fishing area on the river.

From this point the trail climbs back up to Towaliga River Drive. Turn right along the road to return to the trailhead and then cross the road. You now are at the beginning of the Tranquil Trail. Follow this yellow-blazed trail down to a small stream.

After crossing the stream on a small wooden bridge, you next reach the junction at the start of the loop. Go to the right and climb up through a hardwood forest to a ridge with a more level area. Then start a descent into a gully resplendent with Christmas ferns.

As the loop continues, cross two footbridges over small brooks or erosion gullies before reaching a side trail to the right. This path leads to Campground 2 on the river. The path then crosses four more bridges to reach a bench overlooking a tiny waterfall on the right. Soon after this spot, the loop closes. Turn right to climb back up to the trailhead.

Miles and Directions

0.0 Start north at the parking area and cross the Canal Dam.

0.1 Reach the loop trail junction on the right. Continue straight on the trail.

0.2 Cross High Falls Road.

0.3 Arrive at the millstone and old bridge observation site.

0.4 Retrace your steps to the loop junction and turn to the left down the wooden stairs to the two observation decks.

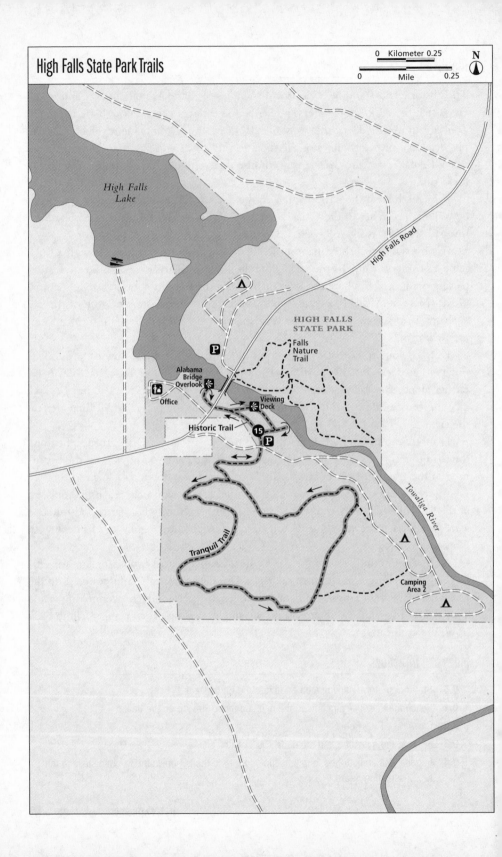

The old millstones and dam on the Towaliga River at the turnaround point on the Historic Trail

0.6 Pass the powerhouse ruins and junction with the connector trail to the fishing area.

0.7 Arrive back at the trailhead on Towaliga River Drive and cross the road on the Tranquil Trail.

0.9 Reach the junction of the Tranquil Trail loop and turn right to walk counterclockwise.

1.2 Hike along the ridge crest at the trail's highest point.

1.3 Reach the fern gullies.

1.4 Cross a footbridge over a fern gully.

1.7 Reach another footbridge.

1.9 Pass the connector trail to Campground 2 on the right.

2.3 After crossing four more footbridges, come to a bench overlooking a tiny waterfall on the right of the path.

2.4 Close the loop and turn right.

2.6 Arrive back at the trailhead.

Options

The **Falls Trail** forms a figure eight with loops at both ends. This 1.2-mile red-blazed trail runs along the northeast side of the Towaliga River, offering good, close views of Towaliga Falls.

16 Chattahoochee Bend State Park Trails

One of Georgia's newest state parks, Chattahoochee Bend opened on 2,910 acres of land in northwest Coweta County in 2011. It also is Georgia's fifth-largest state park. Most of the land has been left in a wilderness setting as it stretches along 5 miles of river shore in a bend of the Chattahoochee.

The park has a visitor center, campground, picnic area, playgrounds, and a boat ramp. Visitors can fish or paddle on the river as well.

Chattahoochee Bend has three trails providing roughly 7 miles of hiking. The East-West (or Tower) Trail runs from the visitor center to the observation deck on the river. The Campground Loop connects with the Riverside Trail. The featured Riverside Trail runs from the boat ramp on the river, upstream to the north paddle-in campground.

Start: At the parking area for the boat ramp on the river
Distance: 9.2 miles out and back
Hiking time: About 2.5–3 hours
Difficulty: Easy
Trail surface: Sandy and forest loam
Best season: Mar–Dec
Other trail users: Hikers only
Canine compatibility: Leashed dogs permitted
Land status: Georgia DNR, State Parks & Historic Sites Division

Nearest town: Newnan
Fees and permits: Daily parking fee
Schedule: Park hours 7 a.m.–10 p.m., year-round
Maps: USGS Whitesburg; full-page map of trails available at the visitor center
Trail contacts: Chattahoochee Bend State Park, 425 Bobwhite Way, Newnan 30263; (770) 254-7271; www.gastateparks.org/chattahoocheebend

Finding the trailhead: From exit 47 near Newnan on I-85, go west 0.6 mile on SR 34 (Bullsboro Boulevard). Turn right onto SR 34 Bypass (Millard Farmer Industrial Boulevard) and drive 6 miles. Turn right at the four-way stop onto SR 34 (Franklin Road). After 8.2 miles, turn right onto Thomas Powers Road. Continue straight for 5.5 miles on this road, which changes names at a couple of intersections. Turn right on Flat Rock Road, which changes to Bobwhite Way and runs into the park. The Riverside Trailhead is at the boat ramp at the end of Bobwhite Way. Trailhead GPS: N33 25.792'/W85 00.671'

The Hike

The Riverside Trail begins at the east side of the boat ramp parking lot, immediately dropping down to cross a small feeder stream. The white-blazed path then turns left toward the riverbank.

As the trail begins following the river upstream, the Chattahoochee is always in sight for the first couple of miles. The trail passes through a forest of beech, water oak, and sweet gum trees. There are a number dead tree snags standing in the river bottom, so the sound of woodpeckers hammering on them is common. Along the

Large patches of mayapples cover the ground along several portions of the Riverside Trail in the early spring.

edges of the sandy path, large and abundant patches of mayapples can be seen in the early spring months.

The trail soon intersects the first of two blue-blazed trails that connect to the campgrounds. A bit farther along, the path reaches a creek crossing, which is the first of seven feeder streams that are encountered along the trail.

Just past the second blue-blazed campground connector entering from the right, another creek crossing immediately appears.

The next landmark that comes into sight is the observation tower and streamside picnic tables. Take a moment to climb the steps up to the top platform of the tower for a view of the river. Along here the Chattahoochee runs deep and several hundred feet wide. One striking feature of the river valley along the Riverside Trail is the quiet. Out of earshot of any roads, you can walk for long stretches without hearing any man-made sound.

After continuing another 150 yards, the blue-diamond-blazed East-West Trail intersects from the right, then 0.4 mile farther the largest of the tributary streams crossed is encountered. Upstream of the bridge, that creek bottom opens into a wide, swampy floodplain.

Beyond this creek the foliage along the trail begins to change. Heavy privet thickets appear along the path, along with yellow poplar trees and loblolly pines. Three more creek crossings are required, and just prior to the last, the trail passes to the right of one of largest beech trees you are ever likely to see. Next the trail reaches a pair of benches at an overlook on the riverbank.

From here the trail turns sharply right and begins climbing up the ridge and parallel to another feeder stream. As the path winds higher, redbuds, hickories, and pines become more common, while beneath there is an understory of buckeye, Christmas ferns, and heartleaf. Meandering around several hardwood coves, the path passes two large rocks jutting out like shelves.

Dropping back down to the river, a side trail leads off to the left and down to a picnic table beside the mouth of a feeder stream. Then the main trail again turns up the ridge side to leave the river. During this climb an old deer stand appears on the right of the trail. Constructed of lumber and mounted with an old boat seat, the contraption is now hanging at an angle from the tree.

Next the trail turns left to run along the edge of a thick, planted pine plantation. The path continues to skirt these evenly spaced rows of trees until reaching a wildlife clearing. After running through the edge of the opening for a short way, the trail reenters the woods to circle all around the rest of the clearing.

When the trail crosses another narrow clearing, it plunges into a pine plantation on the far side. As the path meanders through the rows of trees, it has a mazelike feeling. Pay careful attention to follow the white blazes in this area so you don't miss any and wander off the trail. At the far side of the plantation, the trail ends at the gravel road running down to the paddle-in campground.

This is the turnaround point. Reverse course at the trail-end sign and walk back to the downstream trailhead.

Miles and Directions

0.0 Leave the trailhead, cross the small creek, and turn left toward the river.

0.1 Pass the first connector trail to the campground.

0.4 Reach the second campground connector trail.

0.8 Come to the observation tower.

0.9 The East-West Trail enters from the right.

1.2 Cross the bridge over the largest tributary, with its floodplain to the right.

1.8 Pass the huge beech tree on the left of the path.

1.9 Reach the benches and overlook on the riverbank; the trail turns right up the ridge side.

2.3 Traverse the cove with the rock shelves.

2.5 The trail to the left leads to a picnic table on the riverbank.

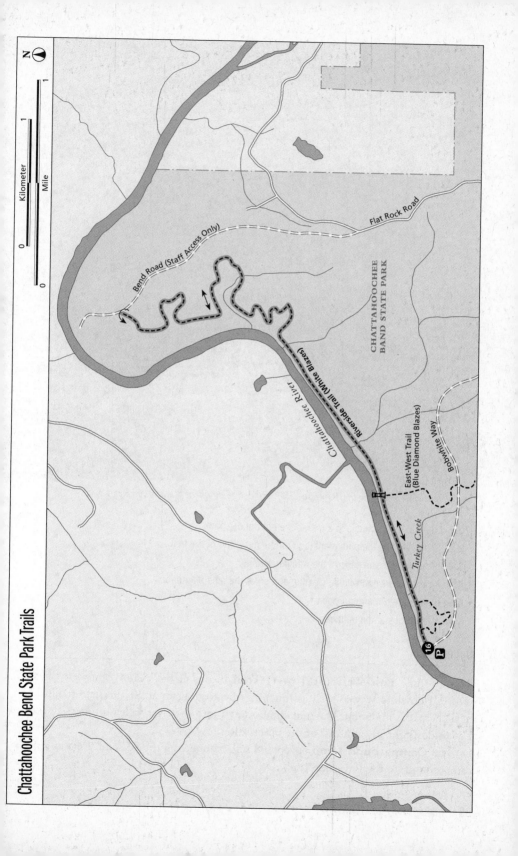

Chattahoochee Bend State Park Trails

N

Kilometer

0   1
Mile

Bend Road (Staff Access Only)

Flat Rock Road

CHATTAHOOCHEE
BEND STATE PARK

Chattahoochee River

Riverside Trail (White Blazes)

East-West Trail (Blue Diamond Blazes)

Bobwhite Way

Turkey Creek

16
P

The observation tower on the Riverside Trail offers a view of the Chattahoochee River.

2.7 The old deer stand is in a tree to the right of the path.

3.2 Begin skirting the pine plantation on the right side of the trail.

3.4 Pass through the edge of the wildlife clearing.

4.3 Cross the second wildlife clearing and enter the pine plantation.

4.6 Reach the turnaround point.

9.2 Arrive back at the trailhead.

Options

The 1.5-mile **East–West (or Tower) Trail** begins at the visitor center. It twice crosses Bobwhite Way, as well as touching the road again at an alternate trailhead near the path's midpoint. The trail climbs down into the river valley to intersect the Riverside Trail 150 yards east of the observation tower.

The **Campground Loop** covers 0.8 mile connecting the RV and walk-in tent campgrounds to the Riverside Trail.

17 | Twin Bridges Trail

The Twin Bridges Trail winds through low, gently rolling ridges and hollows in a mixed hardwood-pine forest on the Little River arm of Lake Sinclair. The impoundment, a Georgia Power Company reservoir on the Oconee River, was built in 1953. The lake's waters are in sight of the trail for most of the hike.

The trail name originates from the pair of bridges crossing sections of the lake in quick succession on the road at the alternate trailhead. The hike begins at the USDA Forest Service Lake Sinclair Recreation Area campground.

Because of the variety of forest and lakeshore habitat, this trail is an exceptionally productive birding area.

Start: At Camp Loop A
Distance: 3.6 miles out and back
Hiking time: About 2 hours
Difficulty: Easy
Trail surface: Soft loam with tree leaves
Best season: Year-round
Other trail users: Anglers; hunters in season
Canine compatibility: Dogs permitted
Land status: Oconee National Forest

Nearest towns: Milledgeville, Monticello
Fees and permits: Daily parking fee charged
Schedule: The campground at the trailhead is closed Dec-Mar.
Maps: USGS Resseaus Crossroads; Oconee National Forest map
Trail contacts: USDA Forest Service, Oconee Ranger District, 1199 Madison Rd., Eatonton 31024; (706) 485-7110; www.fs.usda.gov/conf

Finding the trailhead: From Monticello go east on SR 212 from its junction with SR 16. Continue 17 miles on SR 212 to Twin Bridges Road. Turn left and follow the signs 1.6 miles to the Lake Sinclair Recreation Area entrance, then go to the Camp Loop A parking area. The trailhead is off the road from the parking area at a marker with trail number 119.
From Milledgeville go north 11.2 miles on SR 212 to Twin Bridges Road; turn right and follow directions above. Trailhead GPS: N33 12.260' / W83 24.044'

The Hike

The white-blazed Twin Bridges Trail is marked number 119. This is a fine morning or afternoon hike for campers or day-use visitors. Small streams, the lakeshore, wildflowers, and wildlife add special interest.

Walk down a gentle slope from Camp Loop A and cross the bridge over a small creek at 40 yards. Along the stream are trout lilies, sometimes called dogtooth violets, which bloom in March. Across the bridge, you go through a small thicket of switch cane and into a mature hardwood forest of yellow poplar, oak, and hickory.

The path next crosses a short boardwalk over a damp area and quickly provides the first view of Lake Sinclair, which remains visible for most of the rest of the hike. Several paths leading off to the left are used by anglers to reach the lake for bank

The view of Lake Sinclair at the primitive camping area at the trail end

fishing. Lake Sinclair is a good fishing lake for largemouth bass and crappie. The tree cover extends right to the edge of the water, providing a nice shady place to fish.

The path soon reaches the first of eight short footbridges or boardwalks that dot the remainder of the trail. Only one of these spans a small creek. The rest are over gullies that are remnants of erosion caused by earlier farming. The old gullies have healed with mosses, ferns, trees, and other soil-retention plants.

Wildflowers are well represented throughout the trail. Among those is the pied-mont azalea, with pink flowers on 4- or 5-foot-high bushes blooming in spring. Also look for crane-fly orchids with slender stalks of tiny greenish-yellow flowers blooming in midsummer. Watch for the delicate blooms of blue-eyed grass and tiny yellow blossoms of dwarf cinquefoil in April.

At the fourth bridge a mature yellow poplar is on the left of the trail with a large cavity at the base filled with dirt and decayed wood. Around it and on the facing bank heartleaf, or wild ginger, plants have become established. This small, sweet-smelling plant may last in one place like this for 15 to 20 years.

Tall loblolly pines, little red cedar trees, and dogwoods are along the rest of the trail. The understory has switch cane, as well as the vines of muscadines and greenbrier.

Near the end, the path reaches a dirt road. Turn left on the road and walk to the alternate trailhead at a forest service primitive campground-parking area.

Here you are 0.3 mile from the bridge over the Little River arm of the lake. Across that bridge and another 0.1 mile is the second bridge over Bear Creek.

Twin Bridges Trail

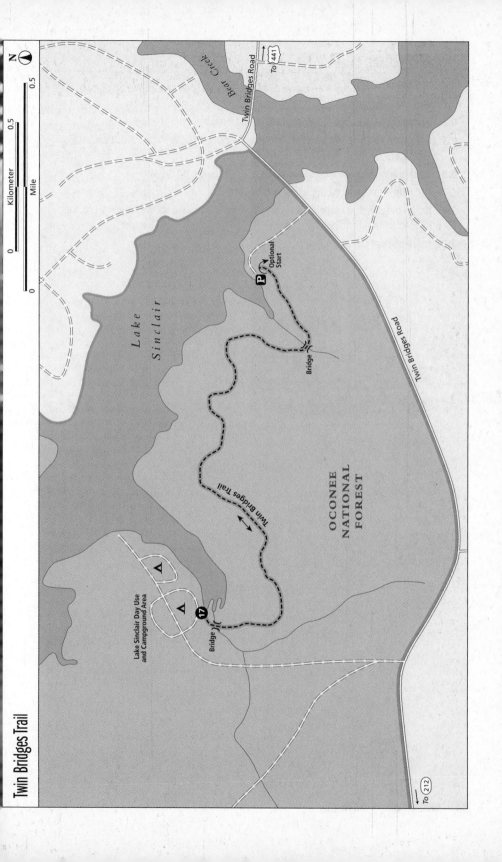

N

Kilometer
0   0.5   0.5

Mile
0   0.5

Bear Creek

Twin Bridges Road

To 441

Lake
Sinclair

Optional
Start

P

Bridge

Twin Bridges Trail

OCONEE
NATIONAL
FOREST

Twin Bridges Road

Lake Sinclair Day Use
and Campground Area

Bridge

17

To 212

Miles and Directions

0.0 Start from Camp Loop A on the white-blazed trail. Walk down a gentle slope to a bridge over a small creek.

0.2 The first view of Lake Sinclair appears on the left.

0.3 Reach the first of the footbridges over erosion gullies that are now healed and well vegetated.

0.5 Cross the bridge with the hollow poplar and wild ginger on the left.

1.7 The path enters a dirt road; follow it to the left.

1.8 Reach the primitive camping and parking area. Turn around for the return hike to the recreation area campground.

3.6 Arrive back at Camp Loop A.

18 DeSoto Falls Scenic Area Trails

The name DeSoto Falls comes from a tale that a piece of armor found near the falls some decades ago belonged to Hernando de Soto or one of his men. Though that expedition traveled through this general area of Georgia in search of gold, the story had been dismissed by historians who doubted such a relic would have survived so long. However, in the late 1920s a portion of an iron Spanish sword was found in an Indian burial mound near Chatsworth to the west. Whatever the truth of the story, the falls have retained the conquistador's name.

To have a look at some of the gold de Soto never found, you can drop in at the nearby Dahlonega Gold Museum or visit Smithgall Woods State Park, where gold was discovered and mined in the 1830s.

There are two waterfalls on this hike, both of which are on tributaries of Frogtown Creek, which runs through the USDA Forest Service's DeSoto Falls Scenic Area. The upper of these two cascades is identified by the forest service as DeSoto Falls, while the other is called Lower Falls. Most visitors combine the hikes to the two falls into a single out-and-back trek.

Start: At the trailhead in the recreation area day-use parking lot
Distance: 2.3 miles out and back
Hiking time: About 1–1.5 hours
Difficulty: Easy
Trail surface: Loamy dirt
Best season: Mar–Dec
Other trail users: Hikers only
Canine compatibility: Dogs permitted; leashed dogs permitted in campground
Land status: Chattahoochee National Forest

Nearest town: Cleveland
Fees and permits: Daily parking and camping fees
Schedule: Trails and campground open year-round
Maps: USGS Neels Gap; USDA Forest Service map of Chattahoochee National Forest
Trail contacts: USDA Forest Service, Blue Ridge Ranger District, 2042 SR 515 West, Blairsville 30512; (706) 745-6928; www.fs .usda.gov/conf

Finding the trailhead: DeSoto Falls Scenic Area is 14.6 miles north of Cleveland on US 129. The trailhead is at the day-use parking lot. Trailhead GPS: N34 42.397'/W83 54.911'

The Hike

This trail takes you through a range of forest types, from the thick rhododendron, mountain laurel, and dog-hobble of the streamsides to a more open hardwood forest of oak, hickory, yellow poplar, maple, and buckeye. Fine spring flower displays begin as early as March and continue with colorful displays of shrubs and trees like silver bell, serviceberry, deciduous magnolias, mountain laurel, rhododendron, and sourwood from April through August. The mountainsides exhibit grand color in mid- to late October.

The Lower Falls Trail runs along Frogtown Creek after leaving the junction with the Upper Falls Trail.

The trail begins at the parking lot, first traversing the camping area to reach the banks of Frogtown Creek. Though small, this creek is stocked with rainbow trout but has some wild fish in it as well.

A picturesque footbridge provides access across Frogtown from the campground. After you cross the bridge, a large wooden sign welcomes you to DeSoto Falls Scenic Area. A smaller sign directs you to the left for the Lower Falls and to the right to DeSoto Falls.

Turn left and walk downstream on the west side of Frogtown Creek. After roughly 100 yards the trail turns away from the creek and begins climbing through a series of switchbacks to reach the unnamed feeder stream just below the Lower Falls. The trail gains about 100 feet of elevation in 0.1 mile as it runs up the cove on the southeast flank of Cedar Mountain. At the foot of the falls, an observation deck provides a good view of the 35-foot cascade.

Return back down the trail, and at the bridge over Frogtown, continue straight on the trail to DeSoto Falls. The path now follows Frogtown Creek upstream through a picturesque area that is abundantly rich in wildflowers during spring. Along the way it crosses one footbridge before turning uphill to the left, away from the stream.

From here to the waterfall the trail gently climbs up into the gap between Rocky Mountain on the north and Cedar Mountain on the south. The path gains almost 100 feet of elevation in the last 0.3 mile.

Just before reaching the falls, the trail crosses a bridge over the unnamed branch on which the cataract is located, and then ends at an observation deck. A vista is provided of the 90-foot series of drops that make up DeSoto Falls.

To complete the hike, return to the bridge over Frogtown Creek and turn left, back to the parking area.

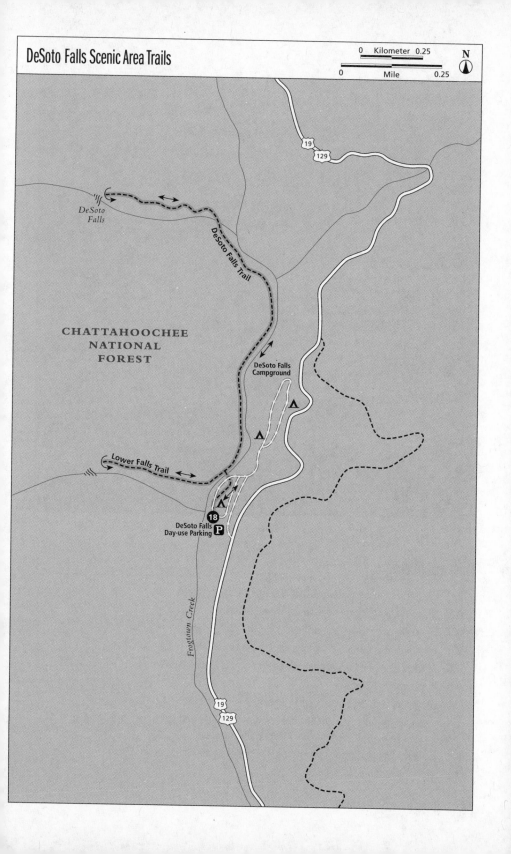

DeSoto Falls Scenic Area Trails

0 Kilometer 0.25

0 Mile 0.25

N

19 129

DeSoto Falls

DeSoto Falls Trail

CHATTAHOOCHEE
NATIONAL
FOREST

DeSoto Falls
Campground

Lower Falls Trail

18

DeSoto Falls
Day-use Parking

Frogtown Creek

19
129

The view from the observation deck at the Lower Falls in the DeSoto Falls Scenic Area

Miles and Directions

0.0 From the trailhead follow the path through the campground.

0.2 Cross the bridge over Frogtown Creek and turn left.

0.3 Leave Frogtown Creek and begin climbing the switchbacks.

0.4 Reach the observation deck for a view of the Lower Falls.

0.6 Arrive back at the bridge; continue straight ahead toward DeSoto Falls.

0.8 Cross a short footbridge.

1.0 Leave Frogtown Creek and begin climbing toward the falls.

1.3 Cross a bridge over the unnamed creek below the falls and reach the observation deck at DeSoto Falls; reverse course back toward the trailhead.

2.1 Back at Frogtown Creek, turn left over the bridge to the campground.

2.3 Arrive back at the trailhead.

19 Smithgall Woods State Park Trails

The 5,604 acres of mountain woodlands here were acquired in 1994 as a gift to the state from conservationist Charles A. Smithgall. The park is dedicated to the purpose of protecting existing landscape, maintaining wildlife diversity, providing environmental education, and permitting low-impact recreational activities.

The prime resource of the park is a stretch of Dukes Creek that runs through the property. This creek is a fine trout stream managed for catch-and-release angling. Trout fishing using artificial lures with barbless hooks is permitted on Wednesday, Saturday, and Sunday.

But it wasn't fish that originally brought people to Dukes Creek. The land along the stream was the site of a gold discovery in 1828 that set off a gold rush 21 years prior to the more famous one in California.

The visitor center is well worth the time spent here. It offers information on the natural and mining history of the property. Besides permits to fish the stream, you can pick up a map of the park and guides to interpretive stations on each of the hiking trails. In all, six relatively short marked trails are laid out to interpret the natural and cultural history of the area.

However, because no private vehicles are allowed beyond the visitor center, getting to the trailheads often involves long walks along the paved or gravel portions of Tsalaki Trail, the main drive through the property.

In addition to the hiking trails, more than 12 miles of paved and unpaved roads are available for walking and bike riding.

The Ash Creek Trail is the featured hike.

Start: At the park visitor center on Tsalaki Trail
Distance: 3.8-mile lollipop
Hiking time: About 1.5–2 hours
Difficulty: Easy to moderate
Trail surface: Dirt; bark chip in a few places; asphalt on Tsalaki Trail
Best season: Mar–Dec
Other trail users: Anglers, bikers, and vehicles on the Tsalaki Trail portion
Canine compatibility: Leashed dogs permitted.
Land status: Georgia DNR, State Parks & Historic Sites Division
Nearest town: Helen
Fees and permits: Daily parking fee

Schedule: Park hours 7 a.m.–10 p.m., year-round; Laurel Creek Trail open year-round; other trails closed during managed hunts
Maps: USGS Cowrock and Helen; page-size map of park with trails available from the visitor center
Trail contacts: Smithgall Woods State Park, 61 Tsalaki Trail, Helen 30545; (706) 878-3087 or (706) 878-3520; www.gastateparks.org/info/smithgall/
Special considerations: Near the end of the Ash Creek Trail, the path crosses Dukes Creek. There is no bridge, and the water usually runs knee deep. Wading is the only option for crossing.

The Hike

The easiest way to hike the green-blazed Ash Creek Trail is to travel clockwise following the twenty markers for the interpretive sites along the path. The tops of these posts are painted lime green and constitute the only blazes along the trail.

Begin by following Tsalaki Trail over a steep ridge and past the Alder Picnic Shelter and Bay's Covered Bridge to the point where the road turns to gravel. The Ash Creek Trail runs off to the right along the gravel drive into the Bear Ridge Camp. Climbing steadily, the trail veers off the left onto a closed and overgrown road just before reaching the camp.

This portion of the path continues steeply through a hardwood forest featuring poplars, white and red oaks, hickories, and maples. Interspersed are some hemlocks

The covered bridge on Tsalaki Trail in Smithgall Woods State Park

Smithgall Woods State Park Trails

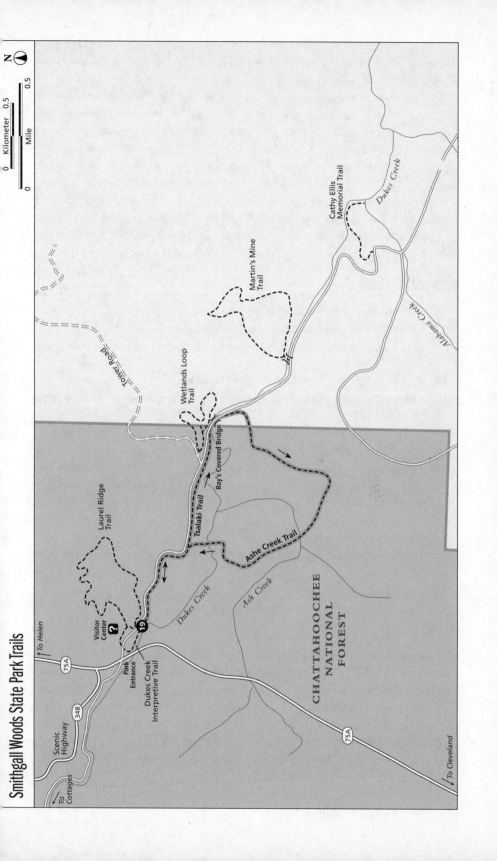

and white pines. Watch for wild violets blooming in the spring, along with patches of mayapple.

On top of Bear Ridge the trail passes through one small and another large wildlife clearing. These feature grasses, clover, sedge, and blackberries. At the end of the second clearing, the trail turns sharply to the right and drops steeply down the ridge.

You next enter a spring bottom lined with New York and Christmas ferns. From there the path runs around the hillside through a tunnel of mountain laurel and rhododendron, before again dropping steeply down to ford Ash Creek.

After climbing a second ridge, the trail descends sharply to reach a ford on Dukes Creek. This is the crossing that requires wading, and the water can be knee deep.

Once across the stream, the trail joins a gravel road around the left side of a planted food plot. Quickly the trail completes the loop when it reaches Tsalaki Trail.

Miles and Directions

0.0 Begin following paved Tsalaki Trail at the visitor center.

0.6 Watch for a line of beehives in the woods to the right of the paved road.

0.7 Pass the junction where the Ash Creek Trail loop closes on the right. Continue down Tsalaki Trail.

1.2 Pass the junction with the Wetlands Loop Trail on the left.

1.4 Pass the Alder Picnic Shelter on the right, cross Bay's Covered Bridge, and turn right up the gravel road.

1.5 Veer left off the gravel road and pass Bear Ridge Camp.

1.7 Enter the first and smaller of two clearings on the ridge.

1.9 Reach the larger clearing.

2.1 At the crest of the ridge, turn right off the old road at the end of the clearing and descend sharply down to a spring bottom.

2.4 Ford Ash Creek.

2.7 Top the crest of the second ridge.

3.0 Ford Dukes Creek and pass to the left of the wildlife food plot.

3.1 Close the loop and turn left on Tsalaki Trail.

3.8 Arrive back at the trailhead.

Options

The **Laurel Ridge Trail** offers the most fascinating nature walk in the park because of its variety of habitats. There are nineteen marked stations along the way, interpreted by a leaflet that discusses features at each waypoint. The 1.5-mile loop trail begins at the paved walkway in front of the visitor center. A large information sign helps orient you to what you may see.

Dukes Creek Interpretive Trail is a short, flat 0.3-mile walk beside a typical mountain trout stream. The trailhead is located at the visitor center on the paved Tsalaki Trail.

Near its end, the Ash Creek Trail requires wading across a ford on Dukes Creek.

The 0.6-mile **Wetlands Loop Trail** is a good example of what happens in this mountain area when water is impounded by either beavers or humans. The trailhead is on Tsalaki Trail, 1.3 miles from the visitor center.

The **Martin's Mine Interpretive Trail** covers 0.9 mile and takes you through the history of early gold mining. Special guided tours are available by advanced registration (check the website for dates). The trailhead is on Tsalaki Trail at a bridge across Dukes Creek, 2.1 miles from the visitor center

The **Cathy Ellis Memorial Trail** is a pleasant 1.0-mile out-and-back walk to a small but beautiful cascading waterfall on Alabama Branch. This trail is also called the Chunanee Falls Trail. A plaque on the trail explains that this is where "gold mining began with the discovery of a gold nugget in 1828 by a slave of Major Franck Logano." The trailhead is on Tsalaki Trail, 2.8 miles from the visitor center on the left.

Local Information

Food/Lodging

Tucked away in a forested wilderness setting, the cottages at Smithgall Woods offer upscale, rustic accommodations. For information and reservations call (800) 864-7275 or visit www.gastateparks.org/info/smithgall.

20 Lake Winfield Scott Recreation Area Trails

Like many other facilities in the Georgia highlands, Lake Winfield Scott and its recreation area were projects constructed by the Civilian Conservation Corps (CCC) in the 1930s. The clear 18-acre lake offers fishing, swimming, and camping. Wildflower and bird viewing are also exceptional here.

Many of the place names in this area hark back to an earlier history. Both Slaughter Creek and Gap, along with nearby Blood Mountain, got their gruesome names from a sixteenth-century battle between Native American tribes that supposedly occurred here. One version names the adversaries as the Cherokees and Creeks, with the Cherokee victory sealing their claim to the Georgia mountains. Unfortunately, with no written history from the period, that remains just one line of conjecture.

The recreation area contains one trail and the opening sections of two others. The Lake Loop Trail is an easy walk encircling Lake Winfield Scott. The Jarrard Gap Trail is a longer, moderate hike from the lake to Jarrard Gap on the Appalachian Trail (AT). The Slaughter Creek Trail, starting at the same trailhead as the Jarrard Gap Trail, also leads to the AT.

The featured trail combines the Slaughter Creek Trail with the Jarrard Gap Trail and up-and-back portion of the AT to Blood Mountain to form a loop.

Start: At the south end of the lake at the information and trailhead signs
Distance: 7.9 mile loop
Hiking time: About 5–5.5 hours
Difficulty: Moderate
Trail surface: Loamy with leaf litter; old roadbeds with dirt and loose rock
Best Season: Oct–June
Other trail users: Hikers only
Canine compatibility: Dogs permitted
Land status: Chattahoochee National Forest

Nearest towns: Blairsville, Dahlonega
Fees and permits: Daily parking fee and recreation area camping fees
Schedule: Open year-round for hiking; recreation area open 7 a.m.–10 p.m. daily.
Maps: USGS Neels Gap; Chattahoochee National Forest map
Trail contacts: USDA Forest Service, Blue Ridge Ranger District, 2042 SR 515 West, Blairsville 30512; (706) 745-6928; www.fs.usda.gov/conf

Finding the trailhead: The entrance to Lake Winfield Scott Recreation Area is 4.3 miles east of Suches on SR 180 and 6.7 miles west of US 129 near Vogel State Park. The trailhead for both Jarrard Gap and Slaughter Creek Trails is on the main entrance road at an information sign and across the road from the parking area on the southeast side of the lake. Trailhead GPS: N34 44.250'/W83 58.370'

The Hike

The Jarrard Gap and Slaughter Creek Trails share a wide path along Slaughter Creek as they leave the trailhead. The trail is marked with light blue blazes.

At the junction with a side trail that goes straight across a footbridge over the creek, the trail turns sharply left and enters a wooded area. After a short stretch along the creek, the path crosses a bridge over the water and comes out onto a gravel road.

The Jarrard Gap Trail splits off, running up the road to the right. Continue straight across the road onto the 2.9-mile-long Slaughter Creek Trail.

The trail passes through a cove hardwood forest, now on the south side of Slaughter Creek. This is a good example of a regenerated hardwood forest that was heavily logged 70 years ago. The path follows blue blazes along an old logging road for much of its distance. As you near the gap, a side trail from the left leads down to the creek and several primitive campsites. Just after this a boundary sign for the Blood Mountain Wilderness Area is at trailside.

After crossing several small streams and springs that are the headwaters of Slaughter Creek, the trail makes the final approach to Slaughter Gap. Along the way the path

The Blood Mountain Trail Shelter is one of the most familiar sights along the Georgia portion of the Appalachian Trail.

The overlook at the top of Blood Mountain is a good place to stop for lunch while enjoying the view.

cuts through a large boulder field to eventually reach the gap at 3,920 feet of elevation. This is 1,050 feet above Lake Winfield Scott. At the gap the Slaughter Creek Trail ends at its junction with the white-blazed Appalachian Trail.

Turn sharply uphill on the AT to the left to continue on to Blood Mountain. The first part of this trail is quite rocky and steep, but it quickly levels out again. You soon pass a pair of side trails to the right that lead to designated primitive campsites.

Next, the junction with the Duncan Ridge Trail appears, approaching from the left. From that point the trail climbs through several switchbacks as it ascends Blood Mountain. When the trail crosses a large stretch of exposed rock, the crest is another 500 feet ahead.

At the top of the 4,461-foot peak, you find the Blood Mountain Trail Shelter. Another product of the CCC, this two-room stone building was built in 1934 and is one of the more elaborate trail shelters on the AT. Climbing to the top of the boulders surrounding the shelter affords sweeping panoramas of the surrounding mountains and valleys from the highest point on the Appalachian Trail in Georgia.

From the top of Blood Mountain, walk back down the AT to the junction with the Slaughter Creek Trail. At the intersection turn left to follow the white blazes of the AT. This trail to the southwest is a gently rolling path, staying on the ridge crest and skirting the mountaintops.

After 0.4 mile the Freeman Trail intersects from the left. The Freeman trail descends for 1.8 miles across the shoulder of Blood Mountain to Flatrock Gap. It also intersects with the 0.7-mile Byron Herbert Reece Trail leading down to the Byron Herbert Reece Farm and Cultural Center. Reece was a noted poet and novelist from Union County in the first half of the twentieth century. His family farm is now open to the public as a museum and arts center on SR 180, just north of Vogel State Park.

Just after the Freeman Trail, a 0.4-mile spur trail leads to the right to the Wood Hole Trail Shelter.

Continuing along on the AT, the path skirts to the west of Turkey Stamp Mountain and passes through Horseshoe Gap. The trail then goes west around Gaddis Mountain to reach Jarrard Gap.

From the gap, turn right on the gravel road and walk 50 yards, following the blue blazes of the 1.3-mile Jarrard Gap Trail to the point it turns left off the road and into the woods. Shortly you cross a wooden footbridge over Lance Branch and begin following that stream gently down its course.

At the foot of the mountain the trail emerges onto gravel Jarrard Gap Road. Turn right on the road and immediately take a left on gravel Slaughter Creek Road. There are blue blazes along the side of the roadway, which takes you to the point at which the loop closes.

Turn left and follow the trail through the woods back to the trailhead and parking lot.

Lake Winfield Scott Recreation Area Trails

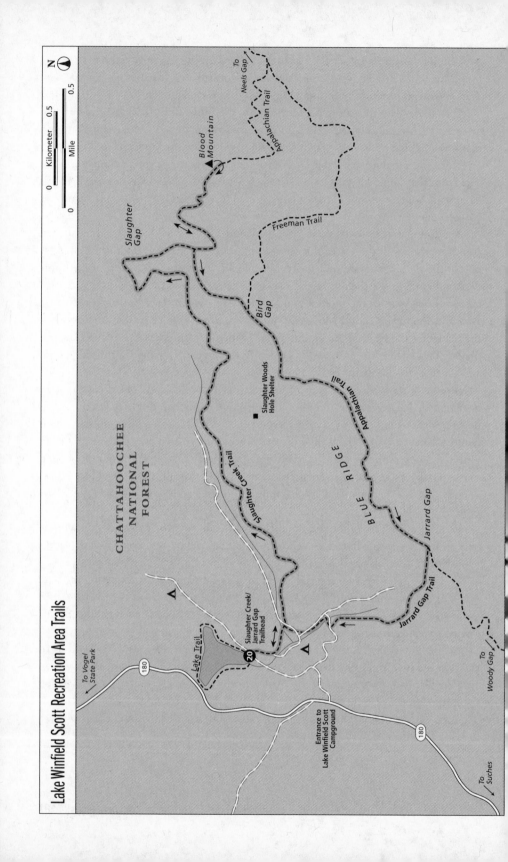

Miles and Directions

0.0 Start at the trailhead parking lot and cross the Lake Winfield Scott dam to the shared trailhead of the Slaughter Creek and Jarrard Gap Trails.

0.2 Turn left into the wood to follow Slaughter Creek upstream.

0.3 Reach the intersection where Slaughter Creek and Jarrard Gap Trails split; continue straight across the road on the Slaughter Creek Trail.

1.8 A connector trail entering from the left leads to a primitive camping area beside Slaughter Creek.

1.9 Reach the boundary sign for the Blood Mountain Wilderness Area.

2.4 Cross the springhead at the origins of Slaughter Creek.

2.7 The trail passes through a large boulder field.

2.9 Reach the junction with the white-blazed Appalachian Trail. Turn left on the AT toward Blood Mountain.

3.3 Pass the junction with the Duncan Ridge Trail on the left.

3.7 Cross an exposed rock face.

3.8 Reach the Blood Mountain Trail Shelter and overlook on the crest of the mountain. Return back down the AT toward the Slaughter Creek Trail.

4.7 At the trail intersection, turn left on the AT toward Jarrard Gap.

5.1 The Freeman Trail intersects from the left, and then the spur to Wood Hole Trail Shelter splits off to the right.

5.5 Pass to the west of Turkey Stamp Mountain.

5.9 Cross through Horseshoe Gap.

6.2 Skirt the west side of the crest of Gaddis Mountain.

6.6 Reach Jarrard Gap and turn right on the blue-blazed Jarrard Gap Trail.

6.9 At the crossing of Lance Branch, begin following the stream down the valley.

7.3 Emerge on Jarrard Gap Road and begin following Slaughter Gap Road.

7.5 Close the loop at the junction with the Slaughter Creek Trail and turn left.

7.9 Arrive back at the trailhead parking lot.

Options

The **Lake Loop Trail** is a 0.4-mile walking path around the clear waters of Lake Winfield Scott. The trail can be accessed from several points, providing good access to walking and fishing.

21 Dukes Creek Falls Trail

Located in the Dukes Creek Falls Recreation Area, this trail provides a trek down into the creek gorge to view several scenic waterfalls. From the trailhead elevation of 2,107 feet, the path drops 340 feet through a pair of long switchbacks. Along the way the trail descends on a broad path with very few steep spots.

The vegetation changes from the well-drained, drier ridgetop of pine and oak, through dense rhododendron and mountain laurel, to the stream edge with large yellow poplar and buckeye trees. An understory of silver bells and dogwoods add their masses of color from early spring into early summer.

Start: Beside the restrooms at the Dukes Creek Falls Recreation Area parking lot
Distance: 2.4 miles out and back
Hiking time: About 1.5 hours
Difficulty: Easy to moderate
Trail surface: Paved to the first observation deck, followed by a short expanse of fine gravel; the lower trail is mostly firm loam.
Best season: Mar–Dec
Other trail users: Hikers only
Canine compatibility: Leashed dogs permitted

Land status: Chattahoochee National Forest
Nearest town: Helen
Fees and permits: Daily parking fee
Schedule: Open year-round, sunrise to sunset
Maps: USGS Cowrock; Chattahoochee National Forest map
Trail contacts: USDA Forest Service, Chattooga River Ranger District, 9975 US 441 South, Lakemont 30552; (706) 754-6221; www.fs.usd.gov/conf

Finding the trailhead: From Helen, go north 1.5 miles on SR 75. Turn left on SR 75 Alternate and go 2.3 miles to Richard Russell Scenic Highway (SR 348). Turn right and go 2 miles; the Dukes Creek Falls parking area is on the left. The trail begins at the south end of the paved parking lot. Trailhead GPS: N34 42.100'/W83 47.347'

The Hike

Before starting down the Dukes Creek Falls Trail, take a moment to look to the southeast. A good view of the distinctively shaped Mount Yonah is afforded from this spot.

The trail begins to the west, traveling along a relatively flat, paved path that leads to an observation deck. This first portion is wheelchair accessible to the overlook. From the deck, a 300-foot cascade can be seen on the opposite side of the gorge. That waterfall is formed by Davis Creek crashing down the cliffs to join Dukes Creek in the creek bottom.

The remainder of the trail is an easy walk into the gorge. From the overlook the trail drops down a set of stairs to a path of fine gravel and loam soil. It is usable in most weather conditions, although rain, ice, or snow might make the footing slippery.

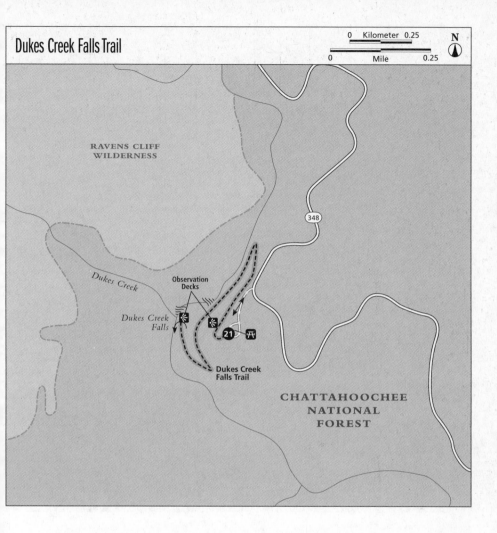

The trail passes through dense rhododendron thickets growing on the very steep gorge slope. About halfway down, the forest changes to the typical cove hardwood trees. On some of the drier sites, oaks, hickories, and Virginia pines dominate. As with many trails in the mountains, spring migrating warblers can be heard as they pass through on their northern flight.

During the descent you first pass a trail junction leading upstream to the Raven Cliffs Wilderness Area and later another for a trail going downstream to Smithgall Woods State Park.

Once at the bottom of the gorge, the trail ends on a set of three connected wooden observation decks. One is directly across the main creek from the foot of the waterfall on Davis Creek. The others provide views of the beautiful cascades, rapids, and pools on Dukes Creek. This stretch of the creek is home to populations of wild rainbow and brown trout.

View of the falls on Dukes Creek

Miles and Directions

0.0   Start at the trailhead beside the restrooms at the parking area.

0.1   Reach the observation deck at the end of the wheelchair-accessible trail.

0.4   At the hairpin curve of the first switchback, the trail to the right connects to the Raven Cliffs Wilderness Area; turn left for the main trail.

0.9   Reach the trail junction for Smithgall Woods State Park at the turn for the second switchback.

1.2   Reach the three observation decks at the end of the trail. The third one overlooks a waterfall on Dukes Creek; this is the turnaround point.

2.4   Arrive back at the trailhead.

22 Pinhoti Trail

The Pinhoti Trail is a 335-mile pathway that runs from Flagg Mountain near Weogufka, Alabama, to a junction with the Benton MacKaye Trail in northwest Georgia near the town of Blue Ridge. The trail enters Georgia in the Ridge and Valley geophysical region of the state, just west of Cedartown. As it progresses to the northeast, it enters the Blue Ridge Mountain region to end in the Cohutta Mountains.

The 145.2 miles of trail in Georgia make the Pinhoti the longest hiking path located entirely within the state. Though the statistics are impressive, they also are misleading. For roughly 60 miles of that distance, the path runs along major roadways, and many more miles are on county or gravel roads. On the actual woodland trails, much of the Pinhoti is on Chattahoochee National Forest lands in the Conasauga Ranger District.

The featured portion of the trail is the most northerly part, which is composed almost exclusively of woodland paths in the Cohutta Mountain region.

Start: At the parking area for the Rock Creek ATV Trail on FS 3A
Distance: 31.6 miles one way
Hiking time: A minimum of 2–3 days
Difficulty: Moderate to strenuous
Trail surface: Dirt and loam in the woodland sections; short gravel road stretches
Best season: Mar–Dec
Other trail users: Hunters in season

Canine compatibility: Dogs permitted; leashed dogs permitted on wildlife management area sections
Land status: Chattahoochee National Forest
Nearest towns: Chatsworth, Ellijay
Fees and permits: None
Schedule: Open year-round
Maps: USGS Talking Rock, Crandell, Dyer Gap, Hemp Top
Trail contact: The Pinhoti Trail Alliance, pinhotitrailalliance.org

Finding the trailhead: From Chatsworth go south on US 76/411 for 5.4 miles. Turn left on US 76 when it splits off to the left. At 100 yards turn right as US 76 joins SR 282. Immediately turn left onto Old Federal Highway. Go 2.3 miles and turn right on Peeple Road. There is no road sign, but a sign for the Rock Creek ATV Trail No. 175 is at the intersection. At 5.7 miles reach the Rock Creek ATV Trail parking area on the left. Trailhead GPS: N34 44.805' /W84 40.509'

The Hike

The original plan in 1925 for the Appalachian Trail called for a spur to run from the Georgia terminus into northern Alabama. Over the years the Pinhoti Trail was developed in the Talladega National Forest of that state, but it did not make the Georgia connection.

The completion of the Benton MacKaye Trail through northwest Georgia in the 1980s spurred renewed interest in the Pinhoti as an Appalachian Trail (AT) connector.

Portions of the Pinhoti Trail in Georgia are blazed with white diamonds bearing a turkey track.

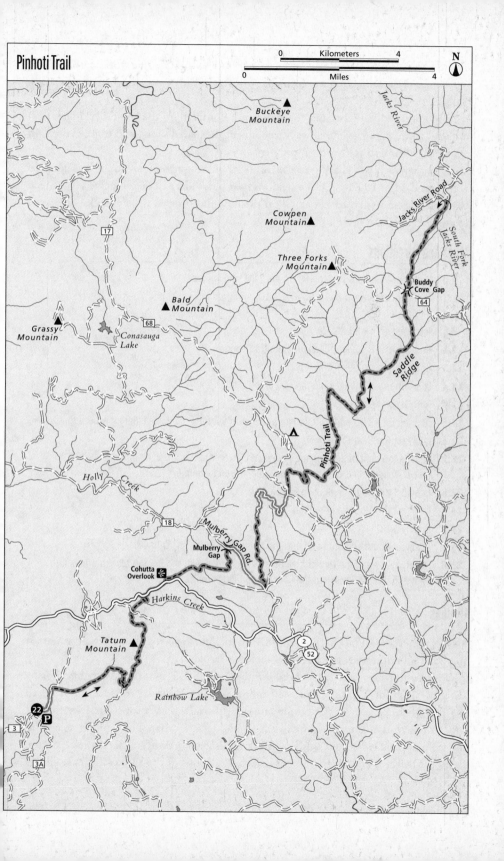

Kilometers

0 — 4

0 — 4

Miles

N

Buckeye
Mountain

Jacks River

Cowpen
Mountain

17

Three Forks
Mountain

Jacks River Road

South Fork
Jacks River

Buddy
Cove Gap

64

Bald
Mountain

Grassy
Mountain

68

Conasauga
Lake

Saddle
Ridge

Pinhoti Trail

Holly   Creek

18

Mulberry Gap Rd.

Mulberry
Gap

Cohutta
Overlook

Harkins Creek

Tatum
Mountain

2

52

Rainbow Lake

22

P

3

3A

The Georgia Pinhoti Trail Association was founded in 1985, and work began on laying out a route connecting the Alabama pathway to the AT via the Benton MacKaye Trail.

Today that route exists, but the trail is not complete in the sense that much of it still uses paved and gravel roadways to connect the actual woodland trail portions. In essence, the Pinhoti is a work in progress.

A variety of blazes mark portions of the trail. A light blue rectangle was adopted as the standard in 2007, but some sections bear older blazes. These may be silver metal or white plastic with a turkey track on them, white painted turkey tracks, or simply white rectangles.

Miles and Directions

0.0 Begin walking northwest on FS 3A from the parking area.

1.1 Turn right onto Rock Creek Road (FS 10) and then follow the trail when it splits off the road to the right.

7.6 Turn east on paved SR 52.

8.1 Turn left off SR 52 and pass the Cohutta Overlook.

12.3 Turn right on Mulberry Gap Road.

13.4 Leave the road to turn onto the trail to the north.

17.0 Turn left on FS 90B.

17.5 Turn left on FS 90 and at 0.2 mile farther, turn left onto a wildlife clearing access road.

21.5 Intersect the Bear Creek Trail.

22.2 Pass to the right of the Gennett Poplar. At 100 feet tall and with a circumference of 20 feet, it is listed as the second-largest tree in North Georgia.

22.6 Intersect the Bear Creek Loop Trail.

24.6 Intersect the Mountain Creek Trail.

28.5 Cross FS 64.

31.3 Intersect South Fork Trail and ford the South Fork of the Jacks River.

31.6 Reach the end of the Pinhoti Trail at the intersection with the Benton MacKaye Trail. Turn right and walk 2.2 miles to the Dyer Gap parking area.

Options

Hikers preferring to tackle the Pinhoti Trail in a north to south direction can start at the trail's junction with the Benton MacKaye Trail.

For the northern terminus of the Pinhoti, from SR 515 in Blue Ridge, go northwest on SR 5 for 3.8 miles. Turn left on SR 2 and follow the road for 9.3 miles to the end of the pavement. Continue another 1.2 miles to Watson Gap. Take the left fork of the road at the gap and drive 3.3 miles to Dyer Gap. The parking area is on the right at the Dyer Gap Cemetery. Walk 2.2 miles north from this trailhead on the Benton MacKaye Trail to the junction at the terminus of the Pinhoti Trail. Trailhead GPS: N34 52.133' / W84 30.880'

23 Lake Russell Recreation Area Trails

The Lake Russell Recreation Area is a USDA Forest Service facility in the eastern section of the Chattahoochee National Forest. The area contains 100-acre Lake Russell and 3-acre Nancy Town Lake. The facility has a 42-site seasonal campground as well.

The Lady Slipper, Lake Russell Foot, Rhododendron, and Sourwood Trails are in the complex, totaling 15 miles in length, plus a partial-loop walking trail around Nancy Town Lake. The featured hike consists of a portion of the Nancy Town Lake walking trail and the Sourwood Trail, forming a 3.7-mile lollipop.

The official Sourwood Trailhead is in the camping area at the north end of the lake, but the road to it is closed from the end of October to the first of April. The parking area at the dam on the south end of Nancy Town Lake is open year-round, providing access to the Sourwood Trail.

Start: At the Nancy Town Lake parking area at the dam
Distance: 3.7-mile lollipop
Hiking time: About 1.5-2 hours
Difficulty: Easy
Trail surface: Dirt and unpaved roadway
Best season: Mar–June; Oct–Dec
Other trail users: Mountain bikes on the Sourwood Trail from the campground to the Nancy Town Road crossing; vehicles and mountain bikes on Nancy Town Lake Road
Canine compatibility: Dogs permitted; must be leashed in the campground

Land status: Chattahoochee National Forest
Nearest town: Mount Airy
Fees and permits: Daily parking fee
Schedule: Trails open year-round; campground and some roads closed Nov–Apr
Maps: USGS Ayersville; page-size maps available from the Chattooga River Ranger District office in Clarksville
Trail contacts: USDA Forest Service, Chattooga River Ranger District, 9975 US 441 South, Lakemont 30552; (706) 754-6221; www.fs.usda.gov/conf

Finding the trailhead: From SR 105 (South Main Street) in Cornelia, take Wyley Street toward Mount Airy for 1.8 miles. Turn right (south) on Lake Russell Road (FS 59) at the Lake Russell Recreation Area sign. Go 1.9 miles and turn left on FS 591, and then right on FS 59H. The parking area and trailhead is at the Nancy Town Lake dam. Trailhead GPS: N34 29.938'/W83 29.026'

The Hike

This is an easy walk past Nancy Town Lake to a small waterfall and beaver pond. The loop portion takes you through a variety of forest habitats, from clear-cuts and new pine plantations to maturing hardwood coves with large yellow poplars, oaks, hickories, and pines. This is an ideal trail for introducing children to a wide variety of plants and animals.

Start at the marker for Trail 152 beside Nancy Town Lake dam. The path drops down to cross Nancy Town Creek immediately below the dam and then climbs up the other side. From this point it skirts the east side of the lake past a large group picnic pavilion. After crossing a footbridge over Nancy Town Creek at the head of the lake, the path reaches a junction at the trailhead for the Lady Slipper Trail.

Stay to the left through the campground and across the bridge at the other end. Turn right onto gravel Nancy Town Lake Road (also called Red Root Road on some maps) and walk 100 yards to the sign marking the beginning of Sourwood Trail loop on the left.

Follow the footpath into the woods as it runs on an old roadbed for about 200 yards along a steep hillside with a noticeable stand of Christmas ferns and mountain laurel. The trail parallels a small branch to the right at the bottom of the hill.

After crossing the branch on a footbridge, the path leads up a gentle slope through loblolly pines before entering a more mature forest. The trail next crosses Nancy Town Road at the highest point on this hike. Mountain bikes are no longer allowed on the trail on the other side of the road.

Beyond the roadway a very open hardwood forest begins, composed of white, chestnut, black, and southern red oaks along with scattered hickories. Look for places in the leaves where turkeys have been scratching in search of acorns and other food. Deer tracks almost always are present in the exposed clay soil of the path.

The path next reaches the junction for a side trail running to the left to Nancy Town Falls. The falls are actually on a small feeder stream of Nancy Town Creek and roughly 100 yards up this trail. Shrouded in dog-hobble and mountain laurel, the water cascades over rock ledges for a total drop of 20 feet.

Returning to the main trail, turn left and follow the small creek downstream past a shallow beaver pond. In late November look for the blue soapwort gentian blooming at the water's edge. Grape ferns, Christmas ferns, and brown-stemmed spleenwort grow along the trail where it passes near the shore.

The pathway continues down the branch past its confluence with Nancy Town Creek, crosses a metal footbridge, and goes down the left bank through laurel and rhododendron. The trail crosses the creek on another bridge, and passes an area where the water cascades over rock ledges just before reaching Nancy Town Lake Road. Turn right on the gravel track, crossing Nancy Town Creek again, and continue along the road. Stay to the left in passing the junction with Nancy Town Road and again when closing the loop.

Miles and Directions

0.0 Start at the trailhead at the Nancy Town Lake parking area.

0.1 Pass the picnic pavilion on the right.

0.3 Cross a bridge over Nancy Town Creek and reach the junction with the Lady Slipper Trail.

0.4 Cross the bridge and turn right on Nancy Town Road; 100 yards farther turn left off the road at the beginning of the loop.

0.7 Leave the creek valley to climb up the ridge to the east.

1.3 Cross Nancy Town Road.

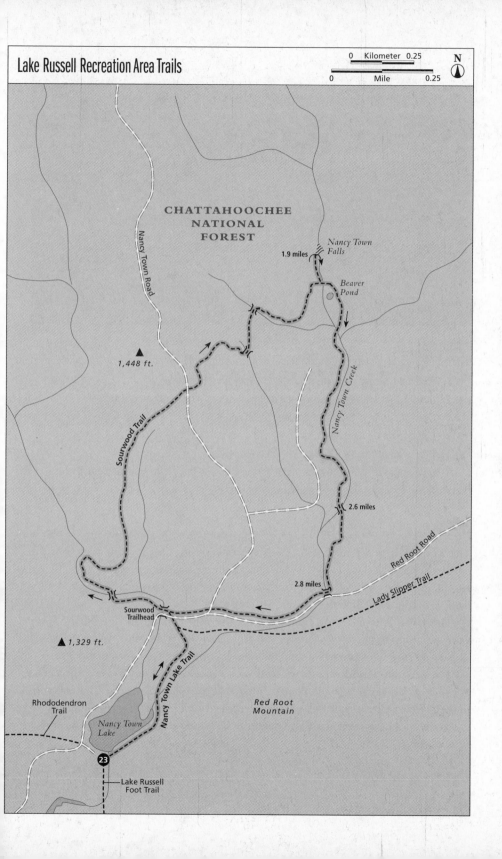

Lake Russell Recreation Area Trails

CHATTAHOOCHEE
NATIONAL
FOREST

Nancy Town Road

Nancy Town Falls

1.9 miles

Beaver Pond

▲ 1,448 ft.

Sourwood Trail

Nancy Town Creek

2.6 miles

Red Root Road

2.8 miles

Lady Slipper Trail

Sourwood Trailhead

▲ 1,329 ft.

Rhododendron Trail

Nancy Town Lake Trail

Nancy Town Lake

Red Root Mountain

23

Lake Russell Foot Trail

N

0   Kilometer 0.25

0   Mile   0.25

The view back across Nancy Town Lake dam to the Sourwood Trailhead

1.8   Reach the junction with the side trail to Nancy Town Falls.

2.1   Cross Nancy Town Creek on a metal bridge and pass a beaver pond on the right.

2.6   Cross Nancy Town Creek on a second metal bridge.

2.8   Come to Nancy Town Road; turn right and cross the creek again.

3.1   Stay to the left at the junction with Nancy Town Road.

3.2   Cross a bridge, close the loop, and retrace the path to the left to return to the trailhead.

3.7   Arrive back at the trailhead and parking lot.

Options

The **Lady Slipper Trail** is a 6.2-mile loop beginning in the campground at the northern end of Nancy Town Lake. This multiuse path is maintained for hiking, mountain biking, and equestrian use. Mostly following old logging roads, the trail is rated as moderately difficult.

The **Lake Russell Foot Trail** begins at the dam parking area on Nancy Town Lake. Running to the southwest, the 4.6-mile loop skirts the shore of Lake Russell and climbs through the surrounding hillsides. The trail is rated easy to moderate.

The 1.5-mile **Rhododendron Trail** was created as an Eagle Scout project. The one-way path begins near the Nancy Town Lake parking area at the dam and runs to the town of Cornelia. It follows an old roadbed for about 200 yards along a steep hillside with a noticeable stand of Christmas ferns and mountain laurel. The trail is rated as easy.

24 Raven Cliffs Trail

This trail in the Raven Cliffs Wilderness Area is one of the more popular hikes in the Georgia mountains. If you want a solitary experience, it is best to walk it during the week or in winter. On weekends from spring through fall, it gets moderately heavy use.

The trail follows a relatively gentle grade along Dodd Creek to Raven Cliffs, which features a waterfall dropping down through a crevice in the tall stone wall.

This is a fine trail for family hiking.

Start: At the trailhead sign at the parking area
Distance: 5.0 miles out and back
Hiking time: About 2.5 hours
Difficulty: Moderate
Trail surface: Dirt with firm loam
Best season: Mar–Dec
Other trail users: Anglers
Canine compatibility: Dogs permitted
Land status: Chattahoochee National Forest
Nearest town: Helen

Fees and permits: None
Schedule: Year-round
Maps: USGS Cowrock; USDA Forest Service map for Chattahoochee National Forest in Georgia
Trail contact: USDA Forest Service, Chattooga River Ranger District, 9975 US 441 South, Lakemont 30552; (706) 754-6221; www.fs.usda.gov/conf

Finding the trailhead: Take SR 75 north out of Helen for 1.5 miles to SR 75 Alternate. Turn left and travel 2.3 miles to the Richard B. Russell Scenic Highway (SR 348). Turn right; after passing the Dukes Creek Recreation Area sign, continue another 0.9 mile and turn left on FS 244. The parking lot is on the left side, and the trailhead is across the gravel road. Trailhead GPS: N34 43.382'/W83 49.398'

The Hike

The trail starts across FS 244 from the parking lot, information kiosk, and restrooms. The path quickly climbs to a bluff overlooking the heavily used primitive camping area at the junction of Dukes and Dodd Creeks. It then drops down to a footbridge over Dodd Creek, just upstream of the creek junction.

The path leads upstream along cascading Dodd Creek in a northwesterly direction toward the cliffs. The creek is home to both wild rainbow and brown trout, so it is not unusual to encounter anglers in the creek or on the path.

The trail alternately brushes up against the stream or climbs 30 to 50 feet above the water level when the steep-sided valley makes it necessary. Although there are no blazes on the trail, it is very easy to follow.

You pass through rhododendron and mountain laurel thickets that form passageways with thick overhead cover. Spring seeps and small brooks cross the trail, making wet places, most of which can be crossed on foot logs.

The massive rock formation of Raven Cliffs towers above the path at the end of the trail.

As the trail climbs following the creek, three major waterfalls appear. The first of these has the creek leaping down a 10-foot drop. Shortly an even more impressive 30-foot cascade is encountered. The third and tallest waterfall before reaching Raven Cliffs is a 70-foot drop on the left of the trail. The hiking path squeezes between that cascade and a rock outcrop on the right.

Large hemlocks, white pines, yellow poplars, deciduous magnolias, hickories, oaks, maples, and buckeyes thrive along the moist valley sides and floor. Under this canopy, a resplendent array of flowering plants bloom throughout early spring, summer, and into late fall. Hepatica, dwarf iris, trout lily, jack-in-the-pulpit, Solomon's seal, various trilliums, foamflower, parasitic squawroot, and one-flowered cancer root start the show beginning in early March. Next come wild geranium, saxifrages, asters, white snakeroot, and mountain mint to finish out the show. Along with spleenworts, bunches of Christmas, New York, beech, maidenhair, and rockcap ferns grow in the valley near the cliffs.

Raven Cliffs Trail

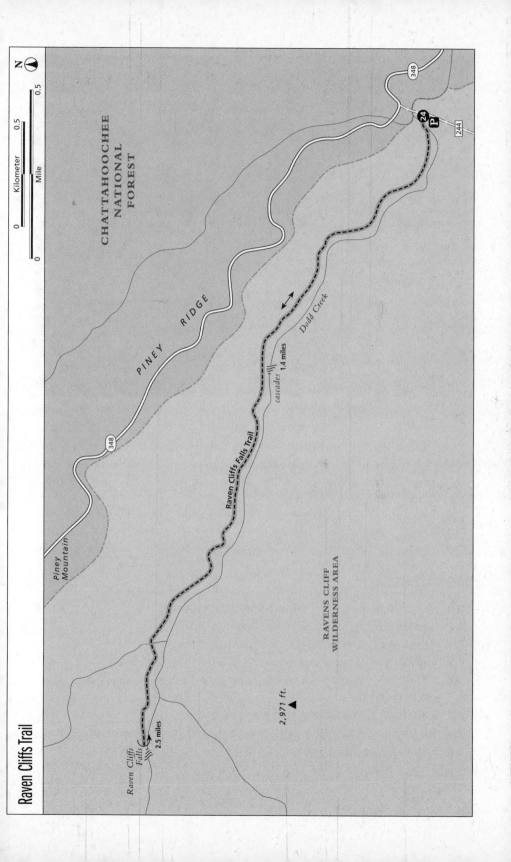

N

CHATTAHOOCHEE
NATIONAL
FOREST

Piney
Mountain

PINEY RIDGE

348

348

Raven Cliffs Falls Trail

Raven Cliffs
Falls

2.5 miles

cascades
1.4 miles

Dodd Creek

2,971 ft.

RAVENS CLIFF
WILDERNESS AREA

24
P

244

0   0.5   Kilometer
0   Mile   0.5

The first bridge across Dodd Creek on the Raven Cliffs Trail

The trail ends below the massive rock face through which Dodd Creek tumbles. That initial drop is 60 feet, plunging through a narrow cleft in the rock wall. From there the creek leaps over a pair of 20-foot drops to complete its passage through Raven Cliffs Falls.

An extension of the main trail climbs precipitously up the mountainside over rough terrain to allow access to the top of the cliffs and views of Dodd Creek valley, 3,620-foot Adams Bald, Wildcat Mountain, and Piney Ridge.

Miles and Directions

0.0 Start at the marked trailhead across FS 244 from the restrooms.

0.2 Cross the footbridge near the junction of Dukes and Dodd Creeks.

0.4 The trail passes close to a 10-foot waterfall on Dodd Creek.

1.2 To the left is an impressive view up toward a 30-foot waterfall on the creek.

1.4 The trail passes between a rock outcrop on the right and a sheer drop down to a 70-foot waterfall on the left.

2.2 Cross a footbridge over a feeder creek joining Dodd Creek.

2.5 Reach the base of the massive rock face and Raven Cliffs. This is your turnaround point.

5.0 Arrive back at the trailhead.

25 Vogel State Park Trails

One of the oldest state parks in Georgia, Vogel is also one of the most scenic. The park is situated on land donated to the state by the Vogel Tanning Company.

Wolf Creek runs through the park and is impounded in the waters of Lake Trahlyta. The impoundment was constructed by the Civilian Conservation Corps (CCC) in the mid-1930s.

Park amenities include campgrounds, a playground, picnic areas, and rental cabins. There is also a minigolf course and paddleboats on the lake. A CCC museum is located on-site as well.

The park's four trails, along with nearby Sosebee Cove Trail, total more than 20 miles and cover a wide variety of conditions and habitats.

Be aware that the Bear Hair and Coosa Backcountry Trails begin at a joint trailhead; both have green blazes. Also, these trails start in the state park, but they also run through lands in the Chattahoochee National Forest. Portions of both trails traverse the Blood Mountain Wilderness Area as well.

The featured hike is on the Coosa Backcountry Trail.

Start: On the drive between the park office and the campground
Distance: 13.2-mile loop
Hiking time: About 2 days if camping, or 1 long, strenuous day hike
Difficulty: Moderate to strenuous
Trail surface: Dirt and old logging roads
Best season: Mar–June; Oct–Dec
Other trail users: Hunters in season
Canine compatibility: Leashed dogs permitted in the state park; dogs permitted on national forest trails
Land status: Georgia DNR, State Parks & Historic Sites Division; Chattahoochee National Forest

Nearest town: Blairsville
Fees and permits: Daily parking fee in the state park; free permit available at the park office for camping on Coosa Backcountry Trail
Schedule: Park hours 7 a.m.–10 p.m. daily, year-round.
Maps: USGS Coosa Bald and Neels Gap; page-size map of park available from the visitor center
Trail contacts: Vogel State Park, 7485 Vogel State Park Rd., Blairsville 30512; (706) 745-2628; www.gastateparks.org
USDA Forest Service, Blue Ridge Ranger District, 2042 SR 515 West, Blairsville 30512; (706) 745-6928; www.fs.usda.gov/conf

Finding the trailhead: Vogel State Park is 11 miles south of Blairsville on US 129. The Coosa Backcountry Trailhead is located about 100 yards from the visitor center on the drive toward the camping areas. Trailhead GPS: N34 45.825'/N83 55.586'

The Hike

The joint trail carrying the Bear Hair and Coosa Backcountry Trails begins with a steady climb along tumbling Burnett Branch. The pathway quickly passes an

The footbridge over the West Fork of Wolf Creek on the Coosa Backcountry Trail

observation deck overlooking Burnett Branch, then the junction with the Byron Herbert Reece Trail. After crossing the branch on a footbridge, you next reach the intersection where the Bear Hair and Coosa Backcountry Trails jointly complete their loops. There is a sign with trail information at this juncture.

Turn right, continuing to follow the path carrying the Bear Hair and Coosa Backcountry Trails. After 70 yards the Bear Hair Trail forks to the left. Turn right, immediately cross a footbridge over Burnett Branch, and climb up to Burnett Gap. In the gap the trail crosses SR 180. The path then runs down the old blocked road that is to the right of the entrance to FS 107. The trail stays on this abandoned road down to the West Fork of Wolf Creek and across it on a footbridge.

Just beyond the bridge the path crosses FS 107 and begins a steady climb. You pass through an impressive rock outcrop prior to reaching Locust Stake Gap. This gap is used frequently as a campsite.

The forest up to this point has been similar to that along the Bear Hair Trail. The forest now is more open, with oaks and hickories dominant. Virginia pines occur on the dry south and west slopes. From here you begin to experience the ridgetop hiking so common in the mountains.

The trail climbs one high, rounded knob after another, only to drop between each one to another gap. You reach Calf Stomp Gap, which is near 3,200 feet, as you cross FS 108. This is about halfway around the loop.

The next mile is a climb to the 4,150-foot contour and the junction with Duncan Ridge Trail, which is marked with blue blazes. The open and flat ridgetop here is another area used frequently as a campsite. If you turn sharply to the right and follow the blue blazes for about 0.25 mile along the Duncan Ridge Trail, you come to Coosa Bald at an elevation of 4,280 feet.

Off the trail to the southwest there is a large rock outcrop. In winter and early spring before the leaves have fully developed, you have an impressive view of the Cooper Creek Valley and the surrounding mountains. Backtracking to the Coosa Backcountry Trail, turn right to follow the green and blue blazes running together all the way to Slaughter Gap.

From Coosa Bald, the trail passes through Wildcat Gap, where it briefly touches FS 39 (Duncan Ridge Road) before climbing up Wildcat Knob. The elevation of the trail here is about 3,800 feet.

The path next drops steeply to Wolfpen Gap and crosses SR 180 again at an elevation of 3,320 feet. This is a good place to leave a shuttle vehicle for breaking the trail into a two-day hike.

From the gap, one of the steepest climbs on the trail winds up onto Duncan Ridge, eventually topping out at 4,145 feet of elevation. During the climb you pass through a boulder field and, as the trail levels out, reach a rock outcrop with a vista to the northeast.

Dropping only slightly into a high gap at more than 4,000 feet, the path then levels out as you go around the east side of Slaughter Mountain. The trail is on an old logging road and is very pleasant, with excellent conditions for spring and early-summer wildflowers. If you are hiking in April, this is also a good place to stop and watch for spring migrating birds. Ravens frequent this high ridge.

At a point due east of the peak of Slaughter Mountain, the trail passes through another boulder field with a good view to the east.

A gentle slope on a long switchback leads down near Slaughter Gap, where the Duncan Ridge Trail splits off to the right to end at the Appalachian Trail. The Coosa Backcountry Trail turns to the east on the left fork at this junction and descends rapidly for about a mile before the Bear Hair Trail enters from the left beside Wolf Creek. Continue along the joint pathway until closing the loop back in the state park. A right turn takes you back to the trailhead.

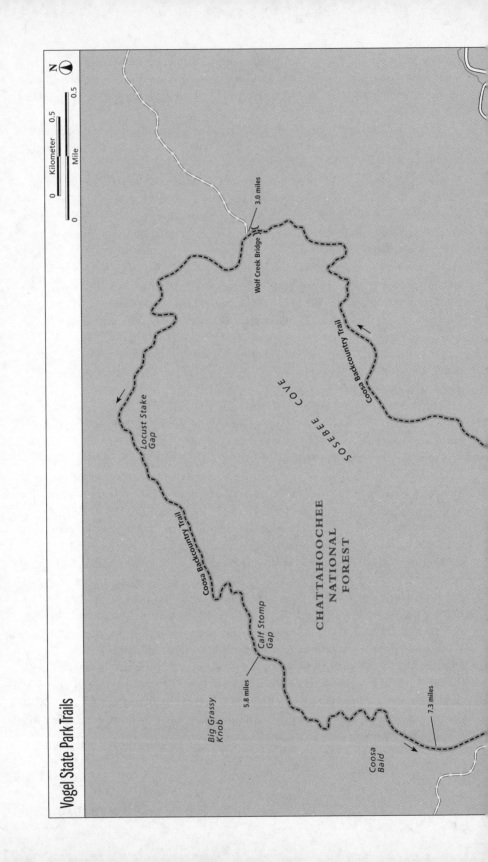

Vogel State Park Trails

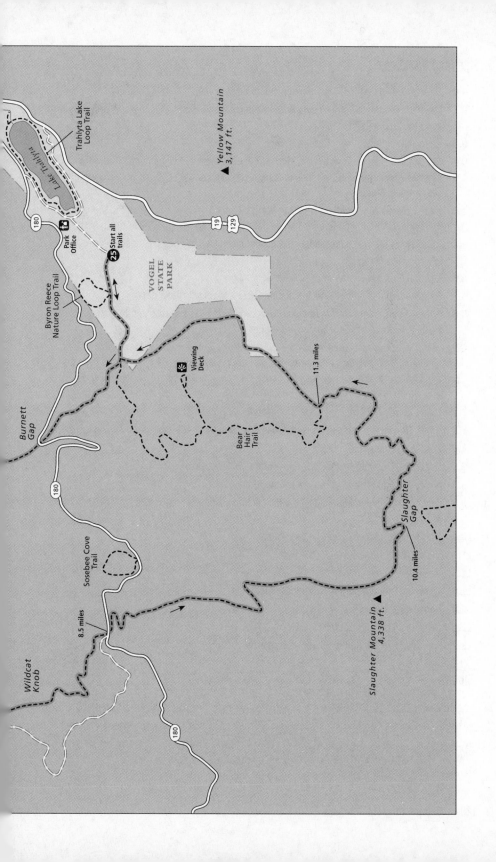

Trahlyta Lake
Loop Trail

Lake Trahlyta

180

Park
Office

25 Start all
trails

Byron Reece
Nature Loop Trail

VOGEL
STATE
PARK

19
129

Yellow Mountain
3,147 ft.

Burnett
Gap

Viewing
Deck

Bear
Hair
Trail

11.3 miles

180

Sosebee Cove
Trail

Slaughter
Gap

10.4 miles

8.5 miles

Wildcat
Knob

Slaughter Mountain
4,338 ft.

180

Miles and Directions

0.0   Start at the shared trailhead with the Bear Hair Trail.

0.1   Reach the observation deck over Burnett Branch; just beyond is the Byron Reece Nature Loop Trail on the right.

0.3   Cross the footbridge over Burnett Branch.

0.4   Reach the intersection where the loop closes from the left. Turn right; at 70 yards pass the junction where the Bear Hair Trail forks to the left. Follow the right fork across a footbridge over Burnett Branch.

1.0   After a steady climb, cross SR 180 at Burnett Gap and follow an old road to the right of FS 107.

3.3   Cross Wolf Creek on a footbridge and quickly cross FS 107; begin a steady ascent in a westerly direction.

4.0   The trail runs through an impressive rock formation.

4.7   Reach a popular campsite at the first ridge crest in Locust Stake Gap.

5.8   Arrive at Calf Stomp Gap at about halfway around the loop; there's another campsite here. Begin walking in a more southerly direction.

6.9   At this relatively level area, reach the Duncan Ridge Trail junction. A sharp turn to the right takes you 0.25 mile on the blue-blazed trail to Coosa Bald at 4,271 feet. Return to the main trail as the Duncan Ridge and Coosa Backcountry Trails run together, with both green and blue blazes.

7.3   Pass through Wildcat Gap, skirting Duncan Ridge Road.

8.5   Cross SR 180 again, this time at Wolfpen Gap, and begin the steepest climb on the loop.

8.6   Pass through a boulder field.

9.1   Reach the crest of Duncan Ridge in another boulder field.

9.2   A rock outcrop offers a good winter vista to the east.

9.8   Cross through a boulder field with a rock outcrop overlook on the east flank of Slaughter Mountain.

10.4   The Duncan Ridge Trail splits off to the right.

11.3   Meet the Bear Hair Trail.

11.6   Cross Wolf Creek on foot logs.

11.9   Leave the Blood Mountain Wilderness Area.

12.0   Reenter the state park.

12.8   Close the loop and turn right.

13.2   Arrive back at the trailhead and parking area.

Options

The **Bear Hair Trail** is a 4.4-mile lollipop that begins and ends using the same pathway as the Coosa Backcountry Trail. This trail then climbs a ridge to the west to reach a spur trail running to Vogel Overlook. From that vantage point an exceptional view of Lake Trahlyta is presented from 900 feet above the water.

The view of Trahlyta Lake from the Vogel Overlook on the Bear Hair Trail

The **Trahlyta Lake Trail** is a comfortable 1.0-mile walk around the lakeshore. A side trail leads to an observation deck below the dam spillway. The bridge over the spillway offers a vista of Blood and Slaughter Mountains that is one of the most photographed in North Georgia.

The **Byron Herbert Reece Trail** is named for the local poet and novelist who owned a farm near Vogel State Park. The farm is now operated by the Byron Herbert Reece Society as a heritage center.

The trail is a short 0.8-mile hike, with interpretive signs along the path describing the interesting natural features of the forest. More species of trees are found on this trail than in all of Yellowstone National Park. The path begins 0.1 mile east of the trailhead along the Coosa Backcountry Trail.

The **Sosebee Cove Trail** is located outside of the state park on national forest property, but it's circled by the Coosa Backcountry Trail. This easy 0.5-mile double loop trail through the 175-acre Sosebee Cove Scenic Area is a memorial to Arthur Woody. Known as the "Barefoot Ranger" for his dislike of footwear, he served as the forest ranger for what is now the Chattahoochee National Forest from 1911 to 1945. He also negotiated the purchase of this area by the federal government.

Situated on the north-facing slope at the very headwaters of Wolf Creek, the cove often has twenty to thirty species of wildflowers in bloom on a single spring day. It also features some of the largest buckeye and yellow poplar trees in the region.

The trailhead and parking area are 3.0 miles west of Vogel State Park on SR 180.

Honorable Mention

B Ocmulgee Bluff Horse, Hike, and Bike Trail System

Composed of more than 30 miles of interconnected multiuse trails, the best hiking venue is the Ocmulgee River Trail. This trail is 3.0 miles of easy walking through the bottomland hardwoods and pines of the Ocmulgee River. The trail is managed by the USDA Forest Service for both hiking and horseback riding.

Explore the riverbank of the historically important Ocmulgee River. Spring wildflowers, birding, wildlife watching, camping, fishing, and small- and big-game hunting in season are all available. What this trail lacks in grand scenery, it makes up in interesting wildlife and wildflower habitat. Deer, raccoons, foxes, gray squirrels, and other mammals are evident from the many tracks left in the soft sandy and silt loam of the riverbank. Wild turkeys, wood ducks, hooded mergansers, woodcocks, quail, and other game birds may be seen or heard. An amazing variety of songbirds use the area as residents and during the spring and fall migrations. Beavers, minks, muskrats, and even an occasional otter may be seen along the river's edge, with turtles sunning on the exposed logs in the river. The hillsides above the floodplain are excellent areas for spring wildflowers. Trout lilies (also called dogtooth violets) bloom on the floodplain in late February and early March.

Interconnected Kinnard Creek and Wise Creek Trails are accessible from the Ocmulgee River Trail. The Kinnard Creek Trail is designated for horseback riding, although hikers are welcome to use the trail. Wise Creek is for both hikers and equestrians.

For more information: Chattahoochee-Oconee National Forests, Oconee Ranger District, 1199 Madison Rd., Eatonton 31024; (706) 485-7110; www.fs.usda.gov/conf
DeLorme: Georgia Atlas and Gazetteer: Page 34 B3

26 Watson Mill Bridge State Park Trails

Watson Mill Bridge State Park is named for the 229-foot covered bridge, constructed in 1880, located at its original site across the South Fork of the Broad River, colloquially known as just South Fork River.

The waterpower from the river at this scenic shoal was once used to drive a gristmill for corn and wheat, a cotton gin, a wool factory, and a woodworking shop. In 1905 the hydroelectric powerhouse, millrace canal, and dam were added. The only remains of this era are the canal that was hewn from the granite wall, along with the powerhouse ruins.

This park has a compact series of four short trails on the south side of the river that exhibit the history of early river life and waterpower. The story is amply told with information boards and pamphlets. The trails provide a good cross section of the numerous habitat types as well. The Bottomland, Powerhouse, South Fork River, and Holly Tree Nature Trails can be combined for the 2.2-mile featured hike.

Additionally, to the north of the river there are 4.75 miles of hiking/biking trails and 12 miles of equestrian paths that can be walked.

Start: At the parking area near the southeast end of the covered bridge and dam

Distance: 2.2 miles out and back, with side loops

Hiking time: About 1.5 hours

Difficulty: Easy

Trail surface: Loamy dirt; walkways, bridges, and steps

Best season: Year-round

Other trail users: Hikers only

Canine compatibility: Leashed dogs permitted

Land status: Georgia DNR, State Parks & Historic Sites Division

Nearest towns: Comer, Elberton, and Athens

Fees and permits: Daily parking fee

Schedule: Park hours 7 a.m.–10 p.m., year-round

Maps: USGS Carlton; small map of the park with the hiking and biking trails available at the park office

Trail contacts: Watson Mill Bridge State Park, 650 Watson Mill Rd., Comer 30629; (706) 783-5349; www.gastateparks.org

Finding the trailhead: From Elberton, go west 13.6 miles on SR 72. At the park sign, turn left (south), cross the railroad track, and immediately turn right on Watson Mill Road. It is an additional 0.7 mile to the park entrance, with the covered bridge 0.4 mile farther south.

The trailhead for the South Side Trails is at the parking area on the east side of the road at the south end of the covered bridge. Trailhead GPS: N34 01.549' / W83 04.458'

The Hike

The South Side Trails are an interconnected system of paths exploring the natural and human history of the park. From the parking lot trailhead below the dam, the path begins on the Powerhouse Trail. At the junction with the Holly Tree Nature Trail, stay

The Watson Mill Covered Bridge and old mill dam, the centerpiece of the state park, is viewed from the Powerhouse Trail.

to the left and cross a footbridge over the millrace canal. Good views are afforded of the covered bridge and dam, with water flowing over the grand shoals below them.

Forty yards farther along, leave the Powerhouse Trail and turn left onto the Bottomland Trail. Here the path descends steeply down wooden steps toward the river. The area is characteristic of the Piedmont Plateau physiographic province and its associated flora. Chain ferns, spleenworts, Christmas ferns, and many spring flowers thrive in the moist riverside habitat. Dog-hobble and mountain laurel are among the shrubs growing in the moist shade. At times the river may overflow parts of this trail.

Large riverine trees—beeches, ironwoods, yellow poplars, sycamores, and water oaks—provide shade during the warm months. An exceptionally large loblolly pine is right beside the trail.

Look for tracks of deer, raccoons, squirrels, beavers, and otters in the soft, sandy soil along the path.

At the junction where the Bottomland and Powerhouse Trails again intersect, turn left on the Powerhouse Trail. The path now follows the millrace canal for 50 yards to cross the dam at the powerhouse ruins. As you walk along the canal, notice the exposed granite walls on both shores. During the warm months you may see frogs and toads as they hop into the canal waterway.

At the powerhouse ruins a connector trail runs to the right to the Holly Tree Nature Trail. The hike continues to the left and is now on the South Fork River Trail.

The well-used South Fork River Trail has no blazes, but it does have directional signs at intersections. It continues downstream for a third of a mile to Pioneer Camp 3 at the mouth of Big Clouds Creek.

Along the way the path passes a large observation deck with excellent views of the river. If you have time to sit here for a while, you may see a wood duck, other water birds, beavers, and turtles.

Next the trail crosses a footbridge over a large gully with a nice view of an attractive cove of hardwood trees and then reaches the lower junction with the Holly Tree Nature Trail on the right. Continuing down the path to the left takes you to the mouth of Big Clouds Creek.

Trees along the trail include beech, ash, hickory, yellow poplar, sycamore, and water oak—all providing food and nesting sites for the animals. Along the way is a variety of flowering plants. Heartleaf and elephant's-foot are visible most of the year. Trilliums, Solomon's seals, false Solomon's seals, trout lilies, and hepaticas bloom here in spring.

When the trail emerges into the pioneer campground, turn left along the gravel road and follow it to the last campsite at the creek mouth. There is no directional sign here, but the trail passes through the campsite and turns to the right, upstream along Big Clouds Creek.

The trail continues up the creek past Pioneer Camp 2 and ends at Pioneer Camp 1. The path passes under a piece of history in the form of the old, abandoned Whitsel Hollow Road steel bridge. Only a few steel bridges of this type are left. The bridge is now covered with vines of muscadine, honeysuckle, and trumpet creeper and provides roosting and nesting places for birds.

Big Clouds Creek flows through a typical bottomland hardwood forest, a productive habitat for plants and animals. There are many animal tracks left by deer, squirrels, beavers, and wild turkeys in the soft sandy-clay path. Thick patches of switch cane grow along the trail.

In places the creek changes character and tumbles over granite boulders. In the quiet water above and below the small cataracts are good places to fish for small bass, sunfish, and catfish.

From Pioneer Camp 1, backtrack to the South Fork River and return upstream. At the junction with the Holly Tree Nature Trail turn left onto that pathway. This trail runs sharply uphill on the ridge side, offering a drier, more upland habitat.

Near the powerhouse ruins a connector trail runs to the right to join the Powerhouse Trail. At this intersection, continue straight on Holly Tree Nature Trail. When the Holly Creek Nature Trail dead-ends into the Powerhouse Trail, turn left to reach the trailhead and the end of the hike.

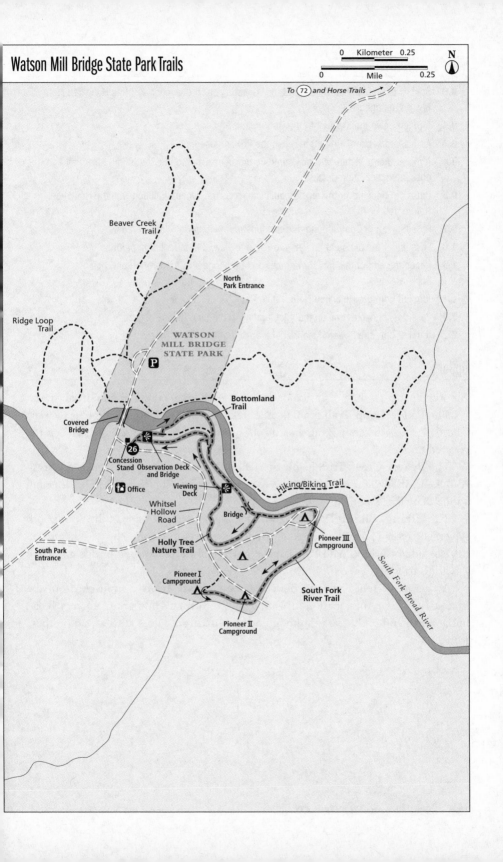

Watson Mill Bridge State Park Trails

0   Kilometer   0.25

0   Mile   0.25

N

To 72 and Horse Trails

Beaver Creek Trail

North Park Entrance

Ridge Loop Trail

WATSON MILL BRIDGE STATE PARK

P

Bottomland Trail

Covered Bridge

26

Concession Stand

Observation Deck and Bridge

Office

Viewing Deck

Whitsel Hollow Road

Bridge

Hiking/Biking Trail

Holly Tree Nature Trail

South Park Entrance

Pioneer III Campground

Pioneer I Campground

South Fork River Trail

Pioneer II Campground

South Fork Broad River

Miles and Directions

0.0 Start at the parking area trailhead; at 70 yards pass the junction with the Holly Tree Nature Trail on the right.

0.1 Turn left down the stairs onto the Bottomland Trail.

0.3 At this intersection, turn left to rejoin the Powerhouse Trail.

0.4 Arrive at the powerhouse ruins; continue downstream onto the South Fork River Trail and pass the observation deck.

0.5 Cross the bridge over the erosion gully and pass the second junction with the Holly Tree Nature Trail.

0.7 Pass Pioneer III Campground and turn upstream along Big Clouds Creek.

1.0 Pass under the old steel bridge, and come in view of Pioneer II Campground.

1.0 Reach the end of this trail turnaround point at Pioneer I Campground and begin backtracking.

1.7 Turn left onto the Holly Tree Nature Trail.

2.0 Pass the connector trail on the right leading to the powerhouse ruins.

2.2 Turn left onto the Powerhouse Trail and arrive back at the trailhead.

Options

All of the paths on the north side of the river are hiking/biking or equestrian trails.

The **Ridge Loop Trail** is a 0.8-mile trek that takes roughly 30 minutes to walk. The trailhead is at the parking area on the west of the road at the north end of the covered bridge.

The **Beaver Creek Trail** begins at a second parking area, a gravel loop off Watson Mill Road, 0.1 mile north of the covered bridge. This trail covers 1.5 miles, forming a loop that takes 1 hour to walk.

The **Hiking/Biking Trail** is a 2.5-mile loop on the north side of the South Fork River. The return portion of the trail parallels the river upstream. The path begins on the east side of Watson Mill Road at the north end of the covered bridge and takes 1.5 hours to walk.

Access to 12 miles of interconnected **Equestrian Trails** is available from the Equestrian Area at the junction of Watson Mill Road and Old Fork Cemetery Road in the north end of the park. Although open to hiking, no dogs are allowed on these paths.

27 Cooper Creek Wildlife Management Area Trails

The Cooper Creek Wildlife Management Area (WMA) covers 30,000 acres of forested mountain ridges within the Chattahoochee National Forest. The property is owned by the US Forest Service, but hunting and fishing are managed by the Georgia Department of Natural Resources. A portion of the WMA around the Cooper Creek Recreation Area campground is designated as the Cooper Creek Scenic Area.

Old timber stands remain untouched, except for a few trees removed many years ago. The 2,160-foot contour runs through the campground near the trailhead. From there, the highest elevation on the featured hike is at 2,963 feet on Yellow Mountain.

The WMA contains a total of five trails offering a bit more than 9 miles of easy to moderate hiking. To a certain extent, confusion reigns on these pathways. All of them are marked with green blazes. Also, signs on the area show the lollipop path through the Cooper Creek Scenic Area as the Cooper Creek Trail. Additionally, the connector path between the Mill Shoals and Yellow Mountain Trails is marked as the Cooper Creek Trail. The latter is referred to here as the Cooper Creek Connector. The other path on the WMA is the Shope Gap Trail.

The featured hike is a Mill Shoals–Yellow Mountain Loop combination composed of all 3.0 miles of the Yellow Mountain Trail and the 0.4-mile Cooper Creek Connector, along with a portion of the 1.7-mile Mill Shoals Trail. This is an out-and-back trek that creates a loop near its beginning and ending point.

Start: At the steps going up the road bank on FS 236, 225 yards west of the Cooper Creek Scenic Area parking lot
Distance: 6.1-mile lollipop
Hiking time: About 2.5 hours
Difficulty: Easy to moderate; a few short, steep grades
Trail surface: Clean loamy dirt with leaf litter
Best season: Mar–June; Oct–Dec
Other trail users: Hunters in season
Canine compatibility: Leashed dogs permitted
Land status: Chattahoochee National Forest
Nearest town: Blairsville

Fees and permits: No fees or permits required for hiking; campsite fees charged mid-Mar to mid-Nov; free camping mid-Nov through Dec
Schedule: Open to year-round hiking; campground closed Jan to mid-Mar
Maps: USGS Mulky Gap; USDA Forest Service Chattahoochee National Forest map
Trail contacts: For marked trails in the Cooper Creek Scenic Area or camping in the Cooper Creek Recreation Area: USDA Forest Service, Blue Ridge Ranger District, 2042 SR 515 West, Blairsville 30512; (706) 745-6928, www.fs .usda.gov/conf

Finding the trailhead: From Blairsville travel west on US 76 to Old US 76; turn left on Old US 76 and go 2.9 miles to Mulky Gap Road. Turn left and follow this winding road 9.9 miles to the Cooper Creek Campground at FS 236; turn left and cross the bridge over Mulky Creek. At 0.5 mile cross the bridge over Cooper Creek and the parking area for the Cooper Creek Scenic Area is on the left. Walk 225 yards back toward the campground on FS 236 for the Mill Shoals Trailhead. Trailhead GPS: N34 45.502'/W84 04.043'

The Hike

The trails of this combination hike follow old logging roads and footpaths through a variety of hardwood, white pine, and hemlock forests, as well as through a variety of conditions, from old stands of large trees to tracts recovering from fire or storm damage.

From the Cooper Creek Scenic Area parking lot, walk west along gravel FS 236 for 225 yards to the Mill Shoals Trailhead. A wooden sign marks the trailhead on the right. Climbing the steps up the road embankment, you begin a steady climb following the green blazes.

The path runs through white pines and hardwoods, with small patches of trailing arbutus and galax at the path's edge. Old American chestnut logs and new sprouts from old stumps are reminders of this great tree that was once dominant on these ridges. The path switches back and forth up a steep ridge with patches of mountain laurel, white pines, chestnut oaks, and several species of ferns.

At the top of the ridge the trail forks; follow the directional sign to the right onto the Cooper Creek Connector for the combination hike. The left fork is the continuation of the Mill Shoals Trail as it follows an old logging road along Mill Shoals Creek for another 0.9 mile to FS 39.

The Cooper Creek Connector climbs over a low ridge and then levels out to a junction, where you turn left onto the Yellow Mountain Trail.

A log bridge carries the trail across Bryant Creek.

Cooper Creek Wildlife Management Area Trails

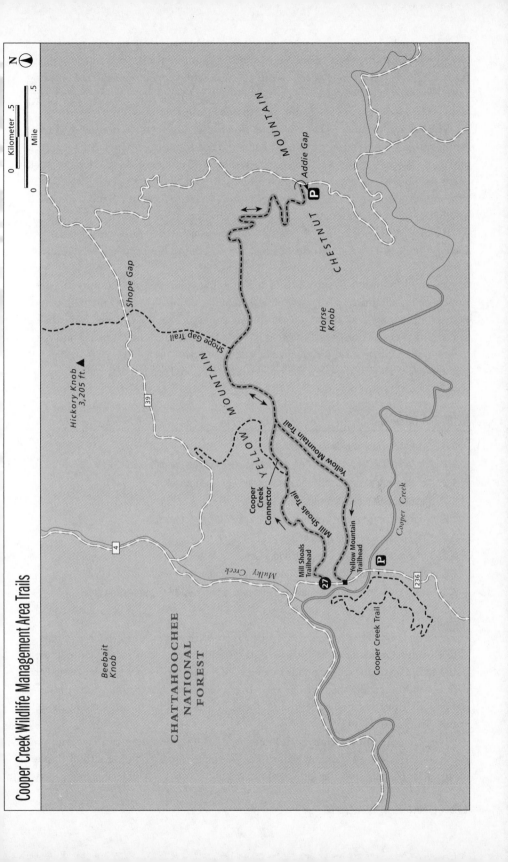

From here to the crest of Yellow Mountain, the hike is on a gentle rolling path for 0.7 mile. Along the way you pass the junction with the Shope Gap Trail entering from the left. At the high point of the trail on Yellow Mountain, you reach a campsite with an excellent vista to the southwest toward Horse Knob.

The Yellow Mountain Trail continues down the ridge crest into a stand of large hemlocks and white pines, switching back and forth until it reaches Bryant Creek and dense growths of rhododendron, dog-hobble, and mountain laurel. Bryant Creek is crossed on a log bridge. In a couple switchbacks you climb the next ridge and then drop into Addie Gap at FS 33A. Just before reaching the forest road, the trail crosses another gravel road running up the hillside.

Retrace your path back to Yellow Mountain and the junction with the Cooper Creek Connector. At the intersection, go left to continue on the Yellow Mountain Trail.

The trail follows the south face of the mountain along a path cut into the steep slope. Trailing arbutus and galax are abundant along this stretch. Next the path begins descending gently down through mountain laurel thickets with some large flame azalea shrubs that bloom April through May. As the trail drops into a hardwood cove, the canopy is composed of yellow poplar and white oaks, then gives way to a stand of white pines as the path reaches the trailhead on FS 236. Turn left and walk along the road back to the parking area.

Miles and Directions

0.0 Start at the Mill Shoals Trailhead sign.

0.7 Turn onto the Cooper Creek Connector that intersects on the right.

1.1 Reach the junction with the Yellow Mountain Trail and turn left.

1.7 The Shope Gap Trail intersects from the left.

1.8 Pass the campsite and overlook at the crest of Yellow Mountain.

2.6 Cross Bryant Creek on a log bridge.

3.1 Arrive at the turnaround point in Addie Gap.

5.0 Turn left at the junction with the Cooper Creek Connector.

6.1 Reach the Yellow Mountain Trailhead and turn left on FS 236 to the parking area.

Options

The **Cooper Creek Trail** has carsonite stakes with arrows at major directional turns in the trail. The trailhead is located across FS 236 from the Cooper Creek Scenic Area parking lot. You cross a small bridge over Tom Jones Branch. A granite stone provides the path's history and designates the trailhead. It is best to begin this walk to the left around the 1.7-mile loop.

The 2.4-mile **Shope Gap Trail** branches off the Yellow Mountain Trail, running north for 0.6 mile to a parking area on FS 39. The path then continues for 1.8 miles more to Mulky Gap and the Duncan Ridge Trail.

28 Piedmont National Wildlife Refuge Trails

The Piedmont National Wildlife Refuge was established in 1939 to manage the wildlife potential of the exhausted farmland. Walking these paths provides a window into the natural and human history of the region.

The area also features a visitor center, the Little Rock Wildlife Drive, and several ponds. An information kiosk provides basic details about the red-cockaded woodpecker and other wildlife on the refuge.

Another sign cautions about ticks, which can transmit Lyme disease and other ailments. Even in cooler weather it is wise to wear protective clothing, tuck pants into footwear, use a strong insect repellent, and check for ticks both during and after the hike.

Three trails are located on the refuge, totaling 4.7 miles of paths. The Red-cockaded Woodpecker, Pine & Creek, and Allison Lake Trails are located near the visitor center.

The featured hike is the Red-cockaded Woodpecker Trail.

Start: At the information kiosk in the parking lot at the end of CR 262
Distance: 2.9-mile lollipop
Hiking time: About 1.5 hours
Difficulty: Easy
Trail surface: Clay loam
Best season: Mar–June; Oct–Dec
Other trail users: Hikers only
Canine compatibility: Leashed dogs permitted
Land status: US Fish and Wildlife Service
Nearest towns: Forsyth, Monticello

Fees and permits: None
Schedule: Open year-round during daylight hours
Maps: USGS Dames Ferry and Hillsboro; trail maps available at the visitor center; Oconee National Forest map
Trail contacts: Refuge Manager, Piedmont National Wildlife Refuge, 718 Juliette Rd., Round Oak 31038; (478) 986-5441; www.fws .gov/piedmont/

Finding the trailhead: From I-75 at exit 186 in Forsyth, travel east on Juliette Road. Go 9.4 miles to a bridge across the Ocmulgee River. Continue on Round Oak Juliette Road 8.2 miles to the refuge visitor center; turn left onto CR 262. The visitor center is 0.5 mile on the right. Continue to the end of the road for the Red-cockaded Woodpecker Trail. Trailhead GPS: N33 06.857'/W83 41.076'

The Hike

The featured Red-cockaded Woodpecker Trail goes through typical pine-hardwood forest to an active nesting site of this small, endangered bird. Benches have been placed so that you can sit quietly to watch for the birds at their nest cavities in live pine trees.

The trail begins at the information kiosk at the end of CR 262. The path quickly passes the start of the Allison Lake Trail on the right and then follows the paved drive

The trail passes the boat landing and fishing pier on Allison Lake.

downhill to Allison Lake. A left turn next puts you on an unpaved service road across the lake's dam.

Nest boxes for wood ducks are placed about the lake and are easily seen from the trail. This area was one of the pioneer places for experimentation with wood duck boxes to improve the population of this most beautiful of our native ducks.

Across the dam the trail continues on the service road for another few yards before turning left into a pine forest on a wide path. Fiberglass posts with hiker symbols mark the path throughout the loop. There also are interpretive signs located along the course of the hike.

As the trail enters wetter sites, oak, yellow poplar, and sweet gum trees replace the pines. The undergrowth of dogwood and occasional redbud trees bloom profusely in early spring. Wildlife along the trail includes deer, foxes, gray squirrels, turkeys, and songbirds.

After crossing a footbridge, reach a bench at the point where the loop portion of the trail begins. The right prong leads to the red-cockaded woodpecker colony; the left prong is the return path to complete the loop.

At 250 yards into the loop the trail crosses a footbridge. Through here watch for erosion gullies that indicate the extent to which this area was farmed during the early 1930s, before it became a national wildlife refuge.

At slightly more than a mile, where the path parallels a dirt road on the right, you reach the mature, towering loblolly pines that are the focal point of the trail. A white ring is painted about 8 feet up on selected trees. These designate the nest trees of the endangered red-cockaded woodpecker. The birds excavate nest cavities in old, live pines that have a fungus disease called red-heart. The small woodpeckers chip away at the bark around the nest cavity, causing the resin to flow down around the tree. The cavities are 15 to 20 feet and higher above the ground.

A bench has been provided for watching the trees for a glimpse of these rare birds. Quiet observation often results in seeing the 8.5-inch woodpeckers, described as zebra-backed with a black cap and a white cheek. They live in family colonies and use the same nest cavity for several years.

The trail next leads away from the nesting colony down to Allison Creek. Wildflowers, ferns, and other plants that prefer moist soils are abundant along the floodplain. The beautiful piedmont azalea grows here, blooming in April and May.

Red-cockaded woodpecker nest trees along the trail are marked with white rings.

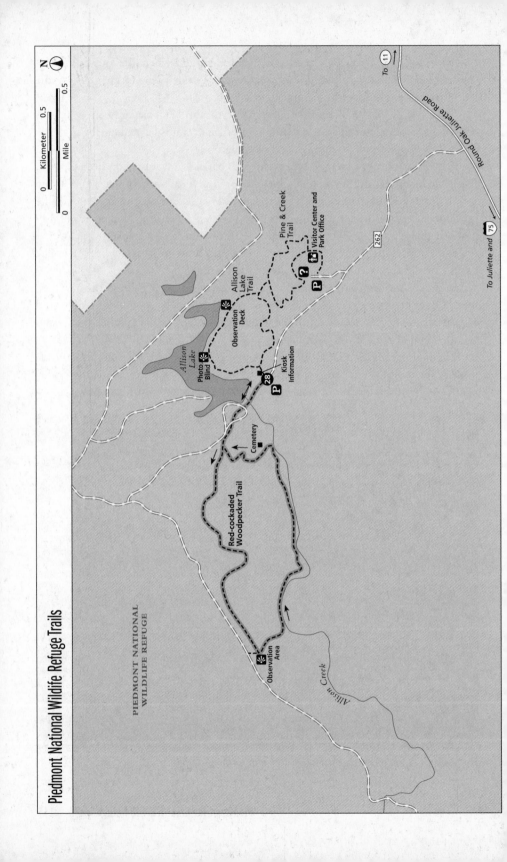

Piedmont National Wildlife Refuge Trails

After crossing another footbridge, keep an eye out for a rock wall off the trail to the right. This is an old cemetery. The graves are marked with stones that are so weathered that no detail is visible.

Upon closing the loop, turn right to walk back to the trailhead.

Miles and Directions

0.0 Start the hike at the information kiosk.

0.3 Leave the service road to follow the trail marked by the fiberglass posts with hiker symbols.

0.6 The trail forks; take the right fork.

0.8 Cross the footbridge.

1.1 Arrive at the benches near the red-cockaded woodpecker nest site. Then follow the trail marker posts, continuing around the loop.

1.6 Reach Allison Creek and walk to the left, upstream along the flow.

1.9 Veer left, leaving the creek, crossing a footbridge, and heading uphill.

2.3 Close the loop and turn right to return to the trailhead.

2.9 Arrive back at the parking area and information kiosk.

Options

The **Pine & Creek Trail** forms a loop beginning at the visitor center and running toward Allison Lake. It is interesting because of the variety of habitats through which it passes.

The 0.9-mile hike begins at a concrete-paved, wheelchair-accessible section 500 feet long. A backyard wildlife habitat demonstration area with a small pool and plantings attracts birds, butterflies, and other animals.

The path then drops down the slope to the creek. The forest changes from a mostly pine canopy to deciduous hardwoods. A bench at a spring invites you to stop and take in the quietness of this pleasant microhabitat.

The Pine & Creek Trail connects to the Allison Lake Trail at an observation deck, before looping back to the trailhead.

The **Allison Lake Trail** begins at the shared trailhead with the Red-cockaded Woodpecker Trail. The 0.9-mile path creates a loop through loblolly pine and bottomland hardwood forests beside attractive Allison Lake. A completely covered photo blind provides an excellent observation point and should be approached quietly.

29 F. D. Roosevelt State Park, Pine Mountain Trail

F. D. Roosevelt State Park is located on Pine Mountain in the central part of the state, about 25 miles northwest of Columbus. The long, narrow ridge composed of quartzite rock formations is the southernmost mountain in Georgia.

Covering 9,049 acres, the tract is Georgia's largest state park and is steeped in the legacy of the thirty-second president. President Roosevelt's Little White House retreat is near the western end of this elongated park, his favorite picnic area on Dowdell Knob is near the midpoint, and the entire park is dotted with facilities built by the Civilian Conservation Corps (CCC) during his administration.

Park amenities are picnic areas, campgrounds, rental cabins, 16 backcountry campsites, equestrian stables, a fishing lake, and swimming pool.

The park contains a total of 47.7 miles of interconnected trails. They are composed of the 23-mile Pine Mountain Trail (PMT), seven connected loops, and half a dozen connectors. The PMT is the centerpiece of trekking in the park, running the entire length from west to east.

Start: At the parking lot on the west end, across US 27 from the Callaway Gardens Country Store

Distance: 23 miles one way

Hiking time: 3 days hiking comfortably at 2–2.5 miles per hour

Trail surface: Dirt and rocky in places; some short sections on paved road

Best season: Mar–June; Oct–Dec

Other trail users: Hikers and backpackers only

Canine compatibility: Leashed dogs permitted

Land status: Georgia DNR, State Parks & Historic Sites Division

Nearest towns: Pine Mountain, Warm Springs

Schedule: Park hours 7 a.m.–10 p.m., year-round

Fees and permits: Daily parking fee

Maps: USGS Pine Mountain and Warm Springs; detailed map of the trails for sale by the Pine Mountain Trail Association (all funds from map sales are used to maintain the Pine Mountain Trail); page-size map of the park including the trail available from the park office

Trail contacts: F. D. Roosevelt State Park, 2970 SR 190, Pine Mountain 31822; (706) 663-4858; www.gastateparks.org

Pine Mountain Trail Association Inc., PO Box 5, Columbus 31902; www.pinemountain trail.org

Finding the trailhead: The eastern trailhead for the PMT is at the paved parking lot and picnic area at the WJSP-TV tower, on US 27/SR 85, just south of Warm Springs. Trailhead GPS: N32 51.173'/W84 42.064'

The western trailhead is at the parking lot at the junction of US 27 and SR 190 across the highway from the Callaway Gardens Country Store. Trailhead GPS: N32 48.650' / W84 51.325'

The Hike

The PMT is the longest single trail in Middle Georgia. The path stretches 23 miles along the crest of the mountain from the towns of Warm Springs in the east to Pine Mountain in the west.

Much of the land through which the PMT passes was originally on a farm owned by President Franklin D. Roosevelt. Today it is part of the state park property.

Combined with its loop and connector trails, 70 miles of treks are possible on the PMT system. These vary from multiday hikes to leisurely family strolls.

Although the trails on Pine Mountain are very much like many of the trails in the highlands of North Georgia, the views seem to be much more panoramic because everything surrounding the mountain is flat. The forest is composed of shortleaf pine,

Several sections of the PMT pass through stretches of tornado damage that devastated the forest.

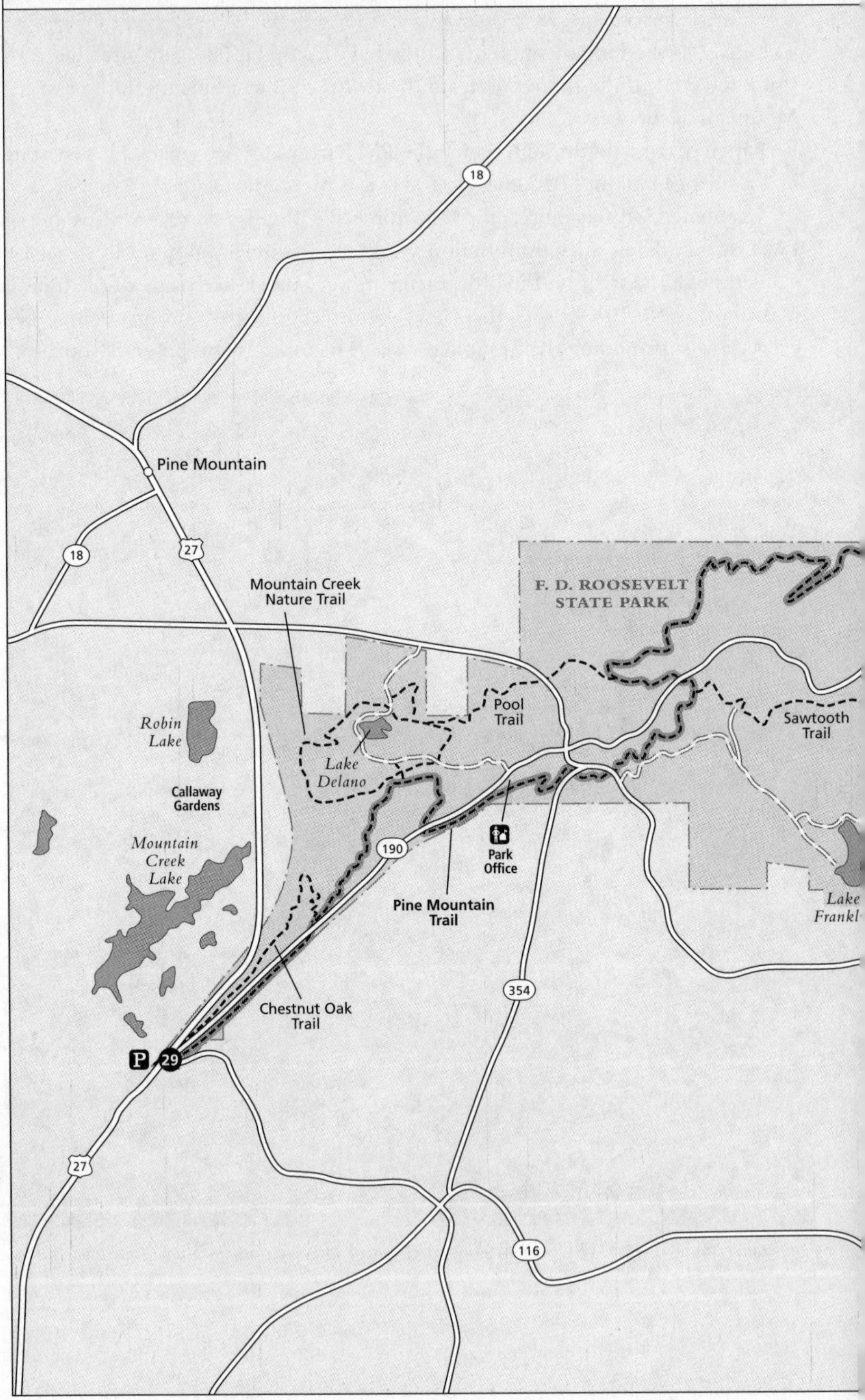

18

Pine Mountain

18

27

Mountain Creek
Nature Trail

**F. D. ROOSEVELT
STATE PARK**

Robin
Lake

Pool
Trail

Sawtooth
Trail

Lake
Delano

Callaway
Gardens

Mountain
Creek
Lake

190

Park
Office

Lake
Frankl

**Pine Mountain
Trail**

354

Chestnut Oak
Trail

P 29

27

116

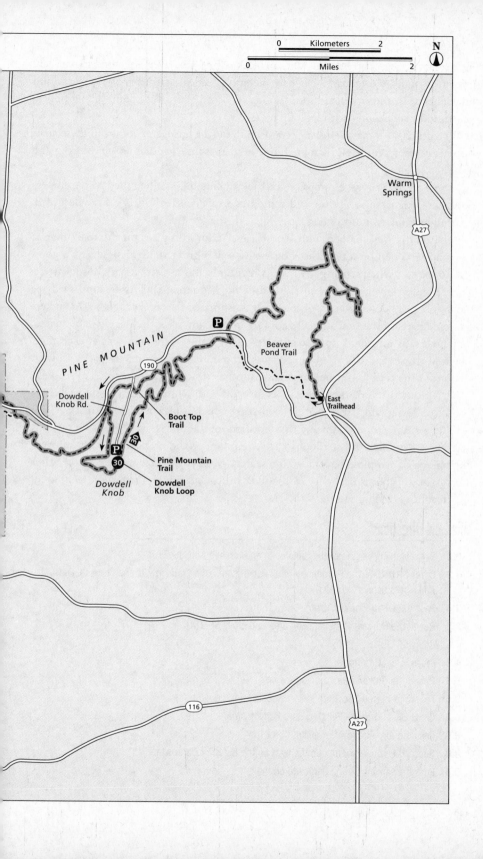

0   Kilometers   2

0   Miles   2

Warm
Springs

A27

PINE MOUNTAIN

190

Beaver
Pond Trail

Dowdell
Knob Rd.

East
Trailhead

Boot Top
Trail

Pine Mountain
Trail

30

Dowdell
Knob

Dowdell
Knob Loop

116

A27

hickory, blackjack oak, chestnut oak, and black oak on the drier ridgetops. The under-growth includes red buckeye, pawpaw, piedmont azalea, sparkleberry, blueberry, and huckleberry. In the coves and moister sites, you can find sweet gum, yellow poplar, beech, and maple along with loblolly pines.

In April 2011 a massive tornado crossed the PMT at several points. In these areas the forest was completely flattened, opening up some panoramic views from the mountain crest.

There are 16 primitive campsites for backpacking hikers along the PMT. Campers must use designated campsites, and campfires are permitted unless otherwise noted. Overnight campers must obtain a permit at the park office.

The trail is well marked with blue blazes. About 100 yards on the trail, there is a green metal box on a post that houses the trail register sheets. It is always a good idea to register when starting the hike. A register is also located at park headquarters. These registers give park personnel and the Pine Mountain Trail Association a tally of the number of people who use the trail. It is estimated that more than 60,000 hikers use some parts of the trail annually, coming from many states and foreign countries.

The trail is measured from west to east with stone cairns and signs at each mile. The trail crosses SR 190 at multiple places, which makes it possible to park and walk sections of the trail from one crossing to another. The Pine Mountain Trail Association has scouted and marked the connector trails with white blazes. The single excep-tion is the Mountain Creek Nature Trail Loop, which is blazed with red marks.

These connectors add greatly to the variety of the long trail. These loop sections make nice day hikes. All the loops have campsites, providing flexibility for an over-night hike and camping in secluded forest areas. Most of the sites are near ample water sources; however, it is necessary to use standard backpacking purification techniques for stream or standing water.

Miles and Directions

0.0 Begin walking west from the parking lot and trailhead on US 27.

1.3 Cross SR 190 at the Garden Overlook Parking Area; the junction with the Chestnut Oak Trail is just across the road.

2.4 Pass the Dead Pine Campsite.

3.2 Reach the Buzzard Roost parking area and cross SR 190.

4.5 Cross SR 354.

4.8 Cross Kings Gap Road.

5.4 Reach the Broken Tree Campsite.

6.0 The white-blazed Sawtooth Trail intersects from the right.

6.2 Cross SR 190 at the Fox Den Cove Parking Area.

6.6 Pass the Turtle Hollow Campsite.

8.0 Reach the connector trail on the right for the Big Knot Campsite.

8.3 Pass the Jenkins Spring Campsite on the left.

9.0 The Beech Bottom Campsite is on the left of the PMT.

11.1 At the Mollyhugger Hill parking lot, cross to the south side of SR 190; the east end of the Sawtooth Trail is on the right just across the road.

11.5 Pass a large rock and a sign for the Whiskey Still Campsite on the right.

13.2 Reach the junction with the west end of the Boot Top Trail on the left.

14.5 Pass the airplane crash monument on the left of the trail.

14.6 The connector trail from the Dowdell Knob parking area enters from the left.

15.9 The Brown Dog Campsite is up a connector trail to the left.

16.3 Pass the east end of the Boot Top Trail.

16.9 The connector trail to the Sparks Creek Campsite is on the right.

17.2 Reach trail on the right to the Big Oak Springs Campsite.

18.0 Cross SR 190 at the Rocky Point parking area.

18.4 Pass the Sassafrass Hill Campsite on the right.

20.3 Reach the Old Sawmill Campsite.

21.5 Pass the Bumblebee Ridge Campsite.

23.0 Reach the eastern trailhead parking lot at the WJSP-TV tower and SR 85 Alternate.

30 F. D. Roosevelt State Park, Dowdell Knob Loop

The Dowdell Knob Loop is a 4.4-mile microcosm of what the loop hikes along the PMT have to offer. Besides being one of the most scenic, it also passes through a couple of the historic locations on Pine Mountain.

The Dowdell Knob overlook affords an impressive panorama. This was one of President Roosevelt's favorite places to go for a cookout. Information plaques tell of his visits.

See map pages 150–151.
Start: In the parking lot at the end of Dowdell Knob Road
Distance: 4.4-mile loop
Hiking time: About 2 hours
Trail surface: Dirt and rocky in places; some short sections on paved road
Best season: Mar–June; Oct–Dec
Other trail users: Hikers and backpackers only
Canine compatibility: Leashed dogs permitted
Land status: Georgia DNR, State Parks & Historic Sites Division
Nearest towns: Pine Mountain, Warm Springs

Fees and permits: Daily parking fee
Maps: USGS Pine Mountain and Warm Springs; detailed map of the trails for sale by the Pine Mountain Trail Association (all funds from map sales are used to maintain the Pine Mountain Trail); page-size map of the park including the trail available from the park office
Trail contacts: F. D. Roosevelt State Park, 2970 SR 190, Pine Mountain 31822; (706) 663-4858; www.gastateparks.org
 Pine Mountain Trail Association Inc., PO Box 5, Columbus 31902; www.pinemountain trail.org

Finding the trailhead: The Dowdell Knob Loop trailhead is 5.6 miles east of the park office. Turn south off SR 190 onto Dowdell Knob Road and drive 1.3 miles to the parking lot at the end of the road. Trailhead GPS: N32 50.434'/W84 44.748'

The Hike

The Dowdell Knob Loop combines the short parking-lot approach trail, a 3.0-mile section of the PMT, and 1.3 miles of the Boot Top Trail. The last trail earns its name from its placement on the loop. The PMT portion of the path creates the outline of a boot, with Dowdell Knob overlook at its southern heel. The Boot Top Trail cuts across the other end, or top of the boot.

There is one campsite along the path, near Mile 16.0 at Brown Dog Bluff.

The hike begins at the Dowdell Knob parking area. Take a few minutes to read the historic markers and see the life-size statue of President Roosevelt that's seated on one of the benches. Also, the barbecue pit he had built on the knob is out on the overlook. The view across King Gap to the south from the overlook is spectacular.

Walk south roughly 90 yards on the connector path leading down to the PMT and turn left to begin the loop along that blue-blazed trail. The pathway passes around the hillside, beneath the overlook. The hike continues to drop down across

The plaque memorializing the crew of the US Air Force bomber that crashed at Dowdell Knob in 1953

the mountainside through a forest of hickory, chestnut oak, and sourwood trees, mixed with a few pines.

The trail then emerges into a large area where the forest is no longer standing but lies twisted and broken on the ground. An F-2 level tornado swept across Pine Mountain around midnight on April 27, 2011. The storm damaged some facilities in FDR State Park and leveled the forests along 4.5 miles of the PMT and its connectors.

The next 0.7 mile of trail is through this huge blowdown. New growth is apparent everywhere as the understory is regenerating with early succession plant life. With the trees downed, views off the mountainside have opened up impressively.

Just after the tornado damage ends, a natural rock wall parallels the left of the trail as the path climbs into a hardwood cove. At the back of the cove the trail fords a small creek beneath a stand of beech and white oak trees with an understory of switch cane. Just past the ford, a side trail leads up the hill on the left to the Brown Dog Bluff campsite.

The path next climbs across the hillside to the junction with the Boot Top Trail. At the intersection, turn left onto the white-blazed pathway. This portion of the hike is on the ridgetop, through an area dominated by oak and pignut hickory trees. Soon a damp springhead bottom full of switch cane is on the left. From here a single, long switchback carries the path up the ridge to cross Dowdell Knob Road.

Once on the west side of the ridge, the trail parallels the headwaters of tiny Bethel Creek to the junction with the PMT. Turn left onto the blue-blazed trail and cross the branch before entering another 0.3-mile stretch of tornado damage. One of the best panoramic views on the hike is provided to the west near the midpoint of this storm clearing.

Once back in the undamaged woodlands, the path begins a steep descent for more than 0.5 mile. Along the way it again passes through 0.3 mile of storm-flattened forests. That damage ends just after the trail starts its final climb back up onto Pine Mountain.

After passing an overlook above private Concharty Lake in King Gap to the south, a plaque appears on the left side of the trail. Near this spot on October 1, 1953, a US Air Force TB-25J twin-engine bomber crashed into the mountain. Flying through rain and fog, the plane had left Eglin Air Force Base (AFB) in Florida, headed to Andrews AFB in Maryland. Only one of the six passengers and crew survived the disaster. The Pine Mountain Trail Association placed the plaque at trailside in a ceremony in November 2012.

Walking another 250 yards completes the loop at the junction with the parking lot connector trail. Turn left to reach the trailhead.

Miles and Directions

0.0 Begin walking south from the trailhead and turn left onto the PMT.

0.2 Pass beneath the Dowdell Knob overlook.

0.5 Enter the area of tornado damage.

1.2 Exit the tornado damage.

1.3 A natural-rock wall parallels the left of the trail up to the creek ford and Brown Dog Bluff connector trail.

1.8 Turn left onto the Boot Top Trail.

2.1 Pass the springhead bottom on the left.

2.4 Cross Dowdell Knob Road.

3.0 Turn left onto the PMT.

3.2 Enter the second storm-damaged area.

3.3 Reach the panoramic view to the west.

3.5 Leave the tornado damage and begin a sharp descent.

3.7 Enter the third storm-damaged area.

4.0 Exit the tornado damage and begin climbing.

4.1 A good view of Lake Concharty in Kings Gap is to the right.

4.2 Pass the plane-crash plaque.

4.3 Close the loop and turn left.

4.4 Arrive back at the trailhead.

Options

The **Mountain Creek Nature Trail** provides a 3.0-mile hike at the foot of the mountain ridge around the park campground, past Lake Delano, and through the vestiges of an old Civilian Conservation Corps fish hatchery. The path also climbs to join a short stretch of the PMT.

The **East End Loop** is the newest of the side trails off the PMT. This 3.4-mile trek is composed of 2.4 miles of the White Candle Trail and parts of the Beaver Pond Trail and PMT. Access is available at the eastern trailhead of the PMT near Warm Springs.

The 6.7-mile **Wolfden Loop** is composed of 1.7 miles of the Beaver Pond Trail and 5.0 miles on the PMT. The trek starts at the WJSP-TV tower at the east end of the PMT. The plant life, rock formations, streams, and waterfalls along the trail make it particularly interesting, and it is considered one of the most beautiful trails in the Southeast. Three primitive campsites—Sassafras Hill, Old Sawmill, and Bumblebee Ridge—are on this loop.

The longest of the loops is the 7.8-mile **Big Poplar Loop,** formed by the 2.7-mile Sawtooth Trail and 5.1 miles of the PMT. Named for a huge yellow poplar located at Mile Marker 10, it runs between Mile Markers 6 and 11 south of SR 190. Big Knot, Beech Bottom, and Grindstone Gap campsites are located on this loop. Access points are at Fox Den Cove and Mollyhugger Hill parking areas.

The **Longleaf Loop** is 6.9 miles long and can be the most confusing of the loops. There are many trail connections, along with seven paved road crossings. It may be started at the Fox Den Cove parking area or at the FDR park office.

The **Overlook Loop** lies at the western end of the PMT. It is a 3.4-mile path formed by 2.1 miles of Chestnut Oak Trail and 1.3 miles of the PMT. Starting points are at the Callaway Country Store and the Gardens Overlook parking areas.

Hike Index

About the Authors

A native of Chattanooga, Tennessee, **Donald W. Pfitzer** retired from the US Fish and Wildlife Service as an assistant regional director of the Southeast Region after 33 years as a fish and wildlife biologist and public affairs officer. He has a master's degree in entomology and botany and has produced thirteen wildlife movies for television for the Tennessee Game and Fish Commission. In 1955 he originated and hosted the first outdoor television program in the Southeast, *Woods and Waters*, and has written many technical and popular articles on fish, wildlife, and nature in general.

Jimmy Jacobs (left), Don Pfitzer (right)

Don is a member and past president of the Southeastern Outdoor Press Association and the Georgia Outdoor Writers Association. He also is a member of the Outdoor Writers Association of America, charter member of the Georgia Conservancy, and a member of the Georgia Hunting and Fishing Hall of Fame. He continues to be active in environmental education, writing, and photography.

Jimmy Jacobs is a lifelong Georgian, born in Atlanta and now living in Marietta. He was the editor of *Georgia Sportsman* magazine for more than two decades and is an outdoor columnist for the *Atlanta Journal-Constitution* newspaper.

A member of the Georgia Outdoor Writers Association and Southeastern Outdoor Press Association, he has authored five guidebooks to fishing the southeastern states and one volume of Southern humor and nostalgia.

About the Photographer

Polly Dean is a native of South Florida, attended the University of Georgia, and never left the state. She makes her home in Marietta. She is an award-winning freelance photographer and writer, as well as a member of the Georgia Outdoor Writers Association and Southeastern Outdoor Press Association.

Polly Dean

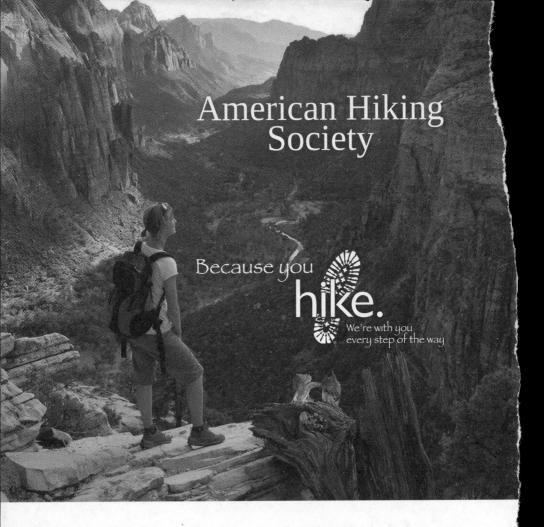

American Hiking Society

Because you **hike.**
We're with you every step of the way

As a national voice for hikers, **American Hiking Society** works every day:

- Building and maintaining hiking trails
- Educating and supporting hikers by providing information and resources
- Supporting hiking and trail organizations nationwide
- Speaking for hikers in the halls of Congress and with federal land managers

Whether you're a casual hiker or a seasoned backpacker, become a member of American Hiking Society and join the national hiking community! You'll enjoy great member benefits and help preserve the nation's hiking trails, so tomorrow's hike is even better than today's. We invite you to join us now!

American Hiking Society

www.AmericanHiking.org • info@AmericanHiking.org